Daily Skill-Builders

Reading

Grades 4–5

Writer
Margaret Gilsenberg

Editorial Director
Susan A. Blair

Project Manager
Erica L. Varney

Cover Designer
Roman Laszok

Interior Designer
Mark Sayer

Production Editor
Maggie Jones

1   2   3   4   5   6   7   8   9   10

ISBN 0-8251-4794-8

Copyright © 2004

Walch Publishing

P. O. Box 658 • Portland, Maine 04104-0658

walch.com

Printed in the United States of America

WALCH PUBLISHING

Table of Contents

Daily Skill-Builders

Reading

Grades 4–5

To the Teacher

Introduction to *Daily Skill-Builders*

The *Daily Skill-Builders* series began as an expansion of our popular *Daily Warm-Ups* series for grades 5–adult. Word spread, and eventually elementary teachers were asking for something similar. Just as *Daily Warm-Ups* do, *Daily Skill-Builders* turn extra classroom minutes into valuable learning time. Not only do these activities reinforce necessary skills for elementary students, they also make skill-drilling an engaging and informative process. Each book in this series contains 180 reproducible activities—one for each day of the school year!

How to Use *Daily Skill-Builders*

Daily Skill-Builders are easy to use—simply photocopy the day's activity and distribute it. Each page is designed to take approximately ten to fifteen minutes. Many teachers choose to use them in the morning when students are arriving at school or in the afternoon before students leave for the day. They are also a great way to switch gears from one subject to another. No matter how you choose to use *Daily Skill-Builders*, extra classroom minutes will never go unused again.

Building Skills for All Students

The *Daily Skill-Builders* activities give you great flexibility. The activities can be used effectively in a variety of ways to help all your students develop important skills, regardless of their level.

Depending on the needs of your students and your curriculum goals, you may want the entire class to do the same skill-builder, or you may select specific activities for different students. There are several activities for each topic covered in *Daily Skill-Builders*, so you can decide which and how many activities to use to help students master a particular skill.

If a student does not complete an activity in the allotted time, he or she may complete it as homework, or you may allow more time the next day to finish. If a student completes a skill-builder early, you may want to assign another. *Daily Skill-Builders* give you options that work for you.

Students in one grade level vary in their abilities, so each *Daily Skill-Builders* book covers two grades. In a fourth-grade class, for example, some students may need the books for grades 3–4. Other students may need the greater challenge presented in the 4–5 books. Since all the books look virtually the same and many of the activities are similar, the students need not know that they are working at different levels.

No matter how you choose to use them, *Daily Skill-Builders* will enhance your teaching. They are easy for you to use, and your students will approach them positively as they practice needed skills.

Guessing Game

I am thinking of an animal that is small and furry. It lives in my house, is chased by the neighbor's dog, and loves tuna fish. Can you guess the animal?

Now, on the lines below, write a description of an animal of your choice. It can be one that lives with you or a favorite zoo animal. **Follow** these **directions.** Include the following: size and shape; color or description, such as hairy, furry, slimy; habitat (where it lives); what it likes to eat. See if your teacher can guess what animal you chose when he or she corrects your paper.

_____

_____

_____

_____

_____

Build an Aquarium!

Did you ever set up a home aquarium? **Follow** the **instructions** to draw all the items in the aquarium below. Before starting, underline all of the words that tell you what to do. These are called the **instruction words.**

1. Draw a layer of stones on the bottom of the tank.

2. Put a castle or a sunken ship in your aquarium.

3. Add some seashells or starfish on top of the stones.

4. Draw some plants on each side.

5. Fill with water.

6. Add three or four fish.

7. Feed your fish!

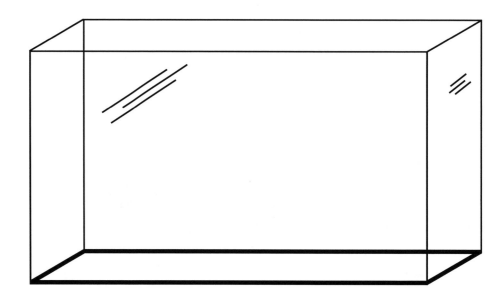

Daily Skill-Builders Reading 4–5
walch.com © 2004 Walch Publishing

Brush Those Teeth!

What should you do every morning and every night? Brush your teeth, of course! Imagine you have a younger brother or sister who is just learning to brush his or her teeth. On the lines below, write detailed **directions** to read to your brother or sister. Make sure you do not skip any steps. Imagine that you can only tell how to do it—you cannot use your hands or any props to show how.

_____

_____

_____

_____

_____

_____

_____

_____

_____

_____

Sandwich Chef

A recipe is a set of **directions.** Directions usually have **instruction words,** or words that tell you what to do. Recipes have a title, a list of ingredients, and directions. Read the following recipe. Underline each instruction word. (**Hint:** Each sentence has at least one instruction word.)

English Muffin Pizza Faces

Ingredients:

3 English muffins	6 black pitted olives,
1 package of grated mozzarella cheese	cut in half
$\frac{1}{2}$ green pepper, cut into thin strips	$\frac{1}{2}$ carrot, sliced into $\frac{1}{2}$"
1 can tomato sauce	rounds

Directions:

Preheat broiler. Separate the muffins into two halves. Toast lightly. Spread $\frac{1}{4}$ cup tomato sauce on each half. Sprinkle with grated mozzarella cheese. Place olive halves for eyes, a thin slice of green pepper for a smiley mouth, and a carrot round for a nose. Put muffins on a baking sheet and broil until cheese melts. Makes 6 servings.

Now, on the lines below, write instructions for making your favorite sandwich. **Remember:** Use instruction words.

(Title) _____

Ingredients: _____

_____

_____

Directions:

_____

_____

_____

_____

_____

_____

Daily Skill-Builders Reading 4–5
walch.com © 2004 Walch Publishing

Five or More a Day

Help friends make good food choices by designing a nutrition poster in the space below. Your **directions** are to include five different fruits or vegetables in five different colors: red, green, yellow, orange, and blue or purple.

GOOD NUTRITION

Diamante Poems

Diamante poems are diamond-shaped and are fun to write. They usually describe two things that are opposites, such as night and day or city and country. One word of the opposites goes on line 1; the other goes on the last line, line 7. Four nouns, two that go with each opposite, are written on line 4. **Follow** the **directions** to create your own diamante poem.

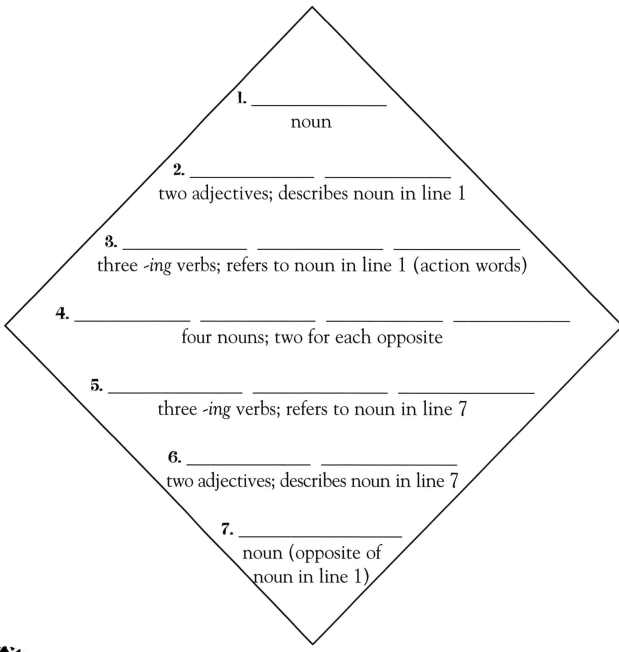

1. _____
   noun

2. _____ _____
   two adjectives; describes noun in line 1

3. _____ _____ _____
   three *-ing* verbs; refers to noun in line 1 (action words)

4. _____ _____ _____ _____
   four nouns; two for each opposite

5. _____ _____ _____
   three *-ing* verbs; refers to noun in line 7

6. _____ _____
   two adjectives; describes noun in line 7

7. _____
   noun (opposite of noun in line 1)

Haiku

A haiku is a short and lovely Japanese poem. It is usually about nature and includes sense words that cause the reader to imagine a scene or feel an emotion. Instead of telling the reader that it is a sunny day, the poet tries to make the reader feel the sun. A haiku usually has three lines. The first line has five syllables, the second line has seven syllables, and the third line has five syllables. Here is a Haiku about spring.

> Lush/ green/ smell/ing/ grass.
>
> Lawn/mow/er/ sounds/ in/ the/ air,
>
> Sneak/ers/ stained/ with/ green.

Think about what senses are affected by the poem. What can you see, feel, taste, smell, or hear from this poem?

Read the haiku below. Separate the syllables.

> Small mouse, gray and white,
>
> Creeping, quivering, stopping.
>
> A cat is prowling.

Now, write a haiku of your own. **Remember:** Check your syllable count.

_____

_____

_____

Solar Quest

Follow directions to label, on the lines provided, the planets of our solar system. Then write the abbreviation of the planet's color in the planet. Sometimes directions are confusing. **Remember:** Double-check the directions, and use a pencil so you can erase any mistakes.

_____

_____

_____

Pluto (brown, BR) is the planet that is farthest away from the Sun.

_____

Our planet Earth (blue, BL) is the third planet from the Sun.

_____

The largest planet is Jupiter (orange, O).

Neptune (turquoise, T) is next to Pluto.

_____

The closest planet to the sun is Mercury (gray, G).

Mars (red, R) is between Earth and Jupiter.

_____

Saturn (yellow, Y) is the planet with big rings.

_____

Venus (white, W) is next to Mercury.

_____

Uranus (aqua, A) is between Saturn and Neptune.

Daily Skill-Builders Reading 4–5
walch.com © 2004 Walch Publishing

Map It Out!

In the space below, draw a map of your town. Be sure to include your house and your school.

Using the map you drew, write **directions** a person can follow to get to your house from your school.

_____

_____

_____

_____

Tanisha Gets Tricked

The story proves that **following directions** can make life easier! Read the following story. Then, on the lines provided, answer the questions below.

One day Tanisha went into her classroom, and the teacher announced, "Today, we will be having a surprise quiz. Please follow the directions carefully! Those who finish first may read a book or use the computers."

The other children moaned and groaned, but Tanisha was happy. She was good at taking tests and quizzes. She knew she could finish first, and then she would have extra time to read her favorite book. She always brought a book to class so she could read when she finished her work. This is what the directions said to do:

Please read all of the questions before starting to work.

Tanisha was in too much of a hurry. There were only ten questions, and she knew she could finish very quickly. She noticed that many of her classmates had finished. Some were giggling and whispering. Some were reading books, while others were using the computers. Tanisha was upset. How did the others get ahead of her? She put her head down and concentrated on finishing. It took her ten more minutes to get to the last question. This is what the last question said:

10. This is not a real quiz. Write your name on the paper and hand it in.

The teacher was smiling when Tanisha handed in her paper. "You are a good student, Tanisha," she said, "But sometimes you don't follow directions."

1. Why did many of the students finish before Tanisha?

_____

_____

2. What should Tanisha have done?

_____

_____

At the Mall

Sequence words tell the order in which things happen. Words such as first, next, finally, and after are sequence words. Underline the sequence words in the following paragraph.

Belinda and Susan's mother agreed to take them to the mall for the afternoon. First, Belinda wanted to buy a candy bar, so they went to Candy Corner. Then, they stopped at Blair's Card Shop to buy Mother's Day cards. Next, Susan wanted to buy a new CD, so they went to the music store. They both wanted to see what was new at Darla's Designs. Then, they spent some time in the bookstore. After that, they looked at the cute puppies at the pet shop. Next, they talked to some friends at Vinny's Video Games. Finally, their mother met them at 5:00 P.M. at the food court for dinner.

List the stores in the order that the girls visited them.

1. _____

2. _____

3. _____

4. _____

5. _____

6. _____

7. _____

Chicken Little's Soup

Read the following story. As you read, think about the **sequence,** or order, of the chores Chicken Little and her animal friends do.

Chicken Little loves vegetable soup. In the spring, she went out to the garden to plant some vegetables. "Who will help me plant?" she asked. "We will!" cried all the other animals. They love vegetable soup, too. They dug up the dirt to make it soft. They planted rows of carrots, corn, beans, and tomatoes.

They went out in the garden all summer and watered the vegetables and pulled up the weeds to give the carrots, corn, beans, and tomatoes space to grow.

In the fall, Chicken Little asked, "Who will help me pick the vegetables?" "We will!" cried all the other animals. When they brought the baskets of carrots, corn, beans, and tomatoes into the kitchen, Chicken Little asked, "Who will help me make the soup?" "We will!" cried all the other animals. They cut up the vegetables and put them in a big pot of boiling water. They took turns stirring the pot. Finally, Chicken Little tasted the soup. It was done. "Who will help me eat the vegetable soup?" she asked. "We will!" cried all the other animals, and they did.

Now, answer the questions below.

1. What do Chicken Little and the other animals have to do in the spring?

   _____

   _____

2. What do Chicken Little and the other animals have to do in the summer?

   _____

   _____

3. What do Chicken Little and the other animals have to do in the fall?

   _____

   _____

Daily Skill-Builders Reading 4–5
walch.com © 2004 Walch Publishing

Maple Syrup Days

Do you like maple syrup on your pancakes? Do you know where maple syrup comes from? Read the following paragraph. Look for the correct **sequence** in the steps for making maple syrup.

If you visit Canada or the northeastern United States in the very early spring, you might see buckets attached to maple trees all through the woods. The freezing and thawing that happens in late February and early March makes the sap flow in these trees. Sap is a watery, sweet, sticky liquid. Farmers put a tap into the maple trees so that the sap will flow into covered buckets. To make syrup, you have to heat the sap so that the water evaporates. It takes many gallons of sap to make one gallon of syrup. After the water has evaporated, the sweet, amber syrup is placed in bottles and sold to consumers. People all over the world enjoy maple syrup!

Put the following steps in the correct order by writing the correct letters in the spaces provided.

1. ____   **a.** You can enjoy maple syrup on your pancakes.

2. ____   **b.** Temperatures rise in late winter or early spring.

3. ____   **c.** Farmers tap the trees and collect sap in a bucket.

4. ____   **d.** The sap is heated in order to evaporate the water.

5. ____   **e.** Syrup is placed in bottles and sold in stores.

Pet Frenzy

Billy has to feed Mrs. Watson's animals while she is out of town. Here is Mrs. Watson's note. Help Billy organize the tasks by putting them in the correct **sequence.**

Dear Billy,

Thank you for feeding my darling pets today. Please don't forget to give Munchkin, the gray kitten, fresh water at 9 A.M. along with one can of cat food. The three dogs—Perky, Pillow, and Pansy—each eat one can of dog food at 5:00 P.M. every day. Mitchell, the parrot, should be fed a cup of birdseed at 2:00 P.M. with a dash of Tabasco sauce on top of the birdseed. Munchkin likes a little cat treat around noon.

The fish need a sprinkle of fish food in the morning. I think that's all!

Thanks,
Mrs. Watson

Time of day	Pet	Instructions
9 A.M.		
12 P.M.		
2:00 P.M.		
5:00 P.M.		

Follow the Leader!

Mr. T. is responsible for organizing the town parade. He needs to make a list so his helpers will be able to organize the floats in the correct sequence. He has decided that the Brass Band should be first, followed by the Recycling float, the High School Drum Majorettes, and then the fire trucks. The Police Chief called to say that his car needs to be first, so the Brass Band will have to be second. The Mayor's wife called to say that the Garden Club float should be last so it will get the most attention. The Scouting float has to go immediately after the Recycling float because Mrs. Wilson has to keep an eye on her daughter, who is the Recycling Princess, and her son, who is with the Scouts. Help Mr. T. make a list of floats for the parade!

Parade Floats

First _____

Second _____

Third _____

Fourth _____

Fifth _____

Sixth _____

Seventh _____

Life Cycle Sequence

Underline each step in the butterfly's life cycle. Pay attention to the **sequence.**

The Life Cycle of the Butterfly

Butterflies have a fascinating life cycle. The females lay tiny, white eggs on the leaves of plants. The eggs hatch into tiny larva or caterpillars, who then eat the leaves. They eat and eat and grow bigger and bigger. Eventually, a caterpillar forms itself into a pupa, or chrysalis. After a while, a beautiful butterfly emerges. The new butterfly drinks nectar from flowers. Butterflies have a short life, but lay eggs on leaves to begin the life cycle again.

Now, write the names of the stages of the life cycle of a butterfly in the correct order.

| pupa | caterpillar |
| butterfly | egg |

1. _____

2. _____

3. _____

4. _____

An Impossible Journey

Read the following story about the Revolutionary Army's capture of Boston. Then number the events below in the correct **sequence.**

If you visit Fort Ticonderoga in New York, you can learn about an exciting event from the American Revolution. In May of 1775, Ethan Allen of Vermont captured Fort Ticonderoga from the British. The next winter, General George Washington had the idea to use the captured cannons from Fort Ticonderoga to drive the British out of Boston. He asked Colonel Henry Knox to bring the cannons to Boston. In December, with the use of boats, the 59 cannons were moved down Lake George. This had to be done quickly before the lake froze. Then, special sleds had to be built so the cannons could be dragged across the snow-covered roads. They had to wait for a snowstorm so the sleds could be used! The cannons were loaded onto the sleds. Knox accomplished what seems today like an impossible task, dragging the heavy cannons 300 miles over lakes, rivers, and mountains in the winter. Knox left Ticonderoga on December 7 and arrived near Boston on January 24, 1776. On March 4, they set up the cannons on the hills above the city. After seeing the cannons looking down on them, the British boarded their ships and left without a fight. It was an important victory for Washington's army.

1. ____   **a.** The cannons are dragged across land to Boston.

2. ____   **b.** A huge snowstorm covers the roads with snow.

3. ____   **c.** The British leave Boston.

4. ____   **d.** Special sleds are built that will carry the cannons.

5. ____   **e.** Fort Ticonderoga is captured from the British.

6. ____   **f.** The cannons are set up overlooking Boston.

7. ____   **g.** The cannons are put on boats and floated down Lake George.

A Shakespearean Sequence

Read the following paragraph about Romeo and Juliet. Pay attention to the **sequence** of the events.

A young man named Romeo decides to disguise himself and go to a ball given by the Capulet family. The Capulets are the sworn enemies of Romeo's family, and Romeo was not invited to the ball. At the ball, Romeo meets Juliet, the daughter of his enemy. They fall in love. The two want to get married, but know that their families will never allow it. They decide to get married secretly and hope for the best. But Juliet's father wants her to marry someone else. So Juliet takes a secret potion that makes it seem as if she is dead. When Romeo finds her, he believes that she really is dead and decides that he doesn't want to live without her. He takes poison and kills himself. Then, when Juliet wakes up, she sees what he has done and decides she cannot live without him. She kills herself. Finally, the families decide to end their fighting, but it is too late for Romeo and Juliet.

Answer the questions below.

1. What happens first in the story? _____

_____

2. What happens at the ball? _____

_____

3. What do Romeo and Juliet decide to do in secret? _____

_____

4. How does Juliet seem after she takes the secret potion? _____

_____

5. What does Romeo do when he thinks Juliet is dead? _____

_____

6. What happens when Juliet wakes up after Romeo kills himself? _____

_____

Your Own Time Line

Time lines are a great way to organize information in the proper **sequence.** Make a time line of your school year. Begin with the day you start school and end with your last day of school. Include holidays, vacations, and special days at school. **Remember:** Organize events in the sequence in which they occur.

My School Year

First day
of school

Last day
of school

Fire Drill

The secretary at your school is trying to type instructions on what to do when the fire alarm goes off. A gust of wind comes through her window and blows her notes all over. Help her put them back in the correct **sequence** by writing the correct letters on the lines provided.

1. ___ **a.** Students line up in alphabetical order in front of teacher outside.

2. ___ **b.** Teacher picks up class list before leaving classroom.

3. ___ **c.** Students line up at door, taking nothing but themselves.

4. ___ **d.** Students walk in a single file line when all-clear bell sounds and teacher signals for them to follow him or her inside.

5. ___ **e.** Students quietly return to classrooms.

6. ___ **f.** When the teacher says it's okay, students quietly leave classroom toward nearest fire exit.

7. ___ **g.** Fire alarm sounds.

8. ___ **h.** Students not with their class at the time of the fire drill leave the building at the nearest exit and immediately notify a teacher.

9. ___ **i.** The first two students to reach the outside doors should hold them for the other students until the teacher reaches the doors.

10. ___ **j.** Students must walk, not run, in single file to assigned fire exit.

11. ___ **k.** Teachers immediately report missing students to principal.

12. ___ **l.** Teachers shut off lights as they leave their classrooms.

13. ___ **m.** Teacher follows students out of classroom, closing door behind him or her.

Topic Talk

A paragraph usually tells about one thing. It is called the **topic.** To find the topic, you can ask yourself, "What is this paragraph mostly about?" The **main idea** mostly tells what the whole paragraph is about. To find the main idea, you can ask yourself, "What is the author mostly saying about this topic?" For each of the following paragraphs, write the topic on the line. Then underline the main idea in the paragraph.

1.   A river is a very important body of water on Earth. Rivers help to transport goods from place to place. Rivers allow people to move from place to place. Rivers allow farmers to water crops. Rivers can even be used to generate electricity.

Topic: _____

2.   Many mammals live and thrive in the Pacific Ocean. Gray whales travel great distances across the Pacific Ocean. Sea otters can often be seen eating and playing off the California coast. Harbor seals are seen by passengers in ships as they sun themselves on large rocks on the surface of the ocean water.

Topic: _____

3.   Do you know what precipitation is? Rain is precipitation. Snow is precipitation. Sleet is precipitation. Did you guess? Precipitation can be any kind of water that falls from the atmosphere.

Topic: _____

Create Topic Sentences

The **main idea** is often represented by a topic sentence. Write a topic sentence for each of the topics below. Your sentence should express a main idea about the topic.

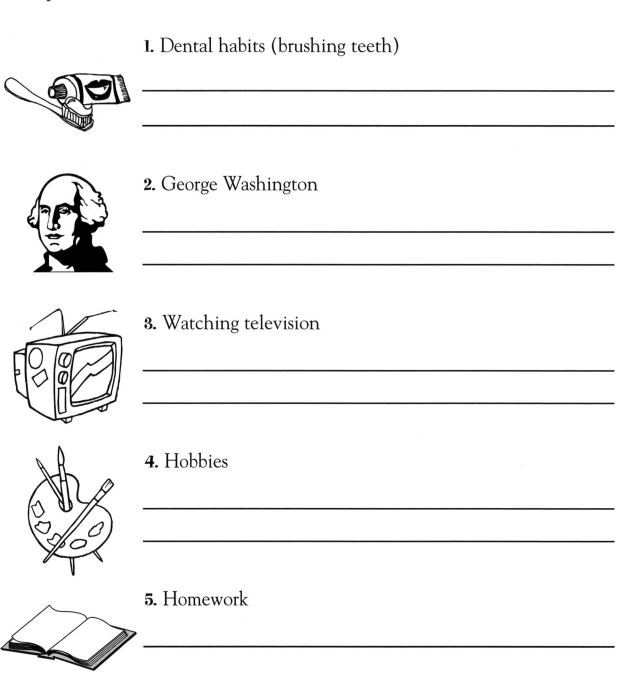

1. Dental habits (brushing teeth)

_____

_____

2. George Washington

_____

_____

3. Watching television

_____

_____

4. Hobbies

_____

_____

5. Homework

_____

_____

Ask Aesop

Fables are stories that teach a lesson. The **main idea** of a fable is the lesson or moral of the story. A man named Aesop, who lived in ancient Greece, wrote a series of moral tales. These are now known as Aesop's Fables.

Read the following modern fable, and underline the main idea, or moral. Then answer the questions below.

> A boy put his hand into a cookie jar. He grasped as many cookies as possible, but when he tried to pull out his hand, it wouldn't fit through the top of the jar. Unwilling to lose his cookies, and yet unable to withdraw his hand, he burst into tears. His sister, who was standing by, said to him, "Be satisfied with half as much, and you will easily draw out your hand." Do not attempt too much at once.

1. What was the boy's problem?

   _____

   _____

2. What choice does he have to make?

   _____

   _____

3. Now, rewrite the moral of the story in your own words.

   _____

   _____

   _____

A Persuasive Idea

Authors have many reasons for writing. Sometimes they want to persuade the reader about something. Persuasive writing can change the way people think and behave. Read the following persuasive paragraph about bats.

> Bats deserve more respect from humans. Bats are mammals—just like us. They are harmless creatures. They are clean and intelligent. Best of all, they help people because they eat lots of mosquitoes.

1. This author is giving information about bats, but the author is also trying to persuade us that bats are helpful to humans. Circle the topic, and underline the **main idea** in the above paragraph. Now rewrite the topic sentence in your own words.

   _____

Read the following persuasive paragraph about cell phones and driving.

> Talking on a cell phone is distracting to a driver. People who are trying to use their phones have to take their eyes off the road. This could cause them to accidentally drive through a stop sign or turn down a one-way street. It only takes a few seconds for an accident to happen and for someone to get hurt.

2. What is the writer trying to tell us?

   _____

3. Circle the topic, and underline the **main idea** in the paragraph. Then rewrite the topic sentence in your own words.

   _____

Reading to Learn

Sometimes authors are writing just to give information about a topic. The **main idea** introduces the subject, as well as what the author is planning to tell us about the subject.

Read the paragraph below, and answer the questions that follow.

Glaciers

How do glaciers move? These massive rivers of ice form in areas where the snow never melts, such as Antarctica or Greenland. One cause of movement is gravity. The packed-down snow gets heavier and heavier until it gradually turns to ice and begins to move under the pressure of its own weight. Glaciers usually move very slowly but can occasionally surge, or move more quickly for a time. This is often caused by melting ice that leaves a layer of water inside the glacier. The water flows faster than ice and moves the whole glacier along. Depending on the climate, glaciers can move forward or backward. Glaciers can carry huge rocks with them and leave the rocks behind when they melt. Scientists learn a lot by studying the movement of glaciers.

---

1. What is the topic of the above paragraph?

   _____

2. What is the author trying to tell us about the topic (What is the main idea)?

   _____

3. Is the author trying to persuade or just inform us?

   _____

4. Write the main idea in your own words.

   _____

Questioning to Learn

When trying to figure out the **main idea** of a paragraph, ask yourself the questions below.

> **Who?** Is the paragraph about a person?
> **What?** What action took place? Or, what is the author telling us?
> **Where?** Is the location mentioned, and is it important?
> **When?** Is the date important?
> **Why?** Is the cause important?
> **How?** In what way was the action accomplished?

Read the paragraph below, and answer the questions that follow.

First Flight

In 1927, Charles Lindbergh made history by flying his airplane, The Spirit of St. Louis across the Atlantic Ocean. Airplanes were still a new technology, and he was the first person to make this flight alone and without stopping. He flew for over 30 hours and had to stay awake the whole time. Lindbergh became a hero when he landed in Paris after flying 3,600 miles. His brave deed proved that airplanes could be a safe way to travel and paved the way for modern aviation.

1. Who? _____

2. What? _____

3. Where? _____

4. When? _____

5. Why? _____

6. How? _____

7. Write a topic sentence that expresses the main idea for the above paragraph. _____

_____

Finding the Main Idea

Read the following paragraph about forest rangers. The paragraph tells about forest rangers, but has no topic sentence.

Protectors of the Forest

To become a forest ranger, one usually has to have a college degree in forestry or in some related field, such as environmental science. Some colleges offer two-year programs in forestry. Most forest or park rangers work at National Parks. Parks that draw large numbers of visitors, such as Yellowstone or the Grand Canyon, employ many rangers. A park ranger's day involves watching out for fires, making sure tourists obey park rules, keeping the park clean, checking plants and animals for diseases, giving tours, or teaching nature classes. Since so many tourists visit the National Parks, rangers have to work with many people.

Use the following questions to help you understand the paragraph, figure out the **main idea,** and develop a good topic sentence.

1. Who? _____

2. What? _____

3. Where? _____

4. When? _____

5. Why? _____

6. How? _____

7. Were you able to answer your questions after reading the paragraph?_____

8. Now write a topic sentence for the paragraph. _____

_____

What's Your Hobby?

The **main idea** in a paragraph is supported by other sentences in the paragraph. Sometimes the main idea is stated. Sometimes it is implied. That is, you have to figure out what the main idea is from the supporting details. Read the following paragraph.

Some people enjoy gardening. They spend all of their free time weeding and planting. They are able to relieve stress by growing plants. Others enjoy bird-watching. They hike in a quiet woodland, trying to spot new birds. Hours spent in the fresh air can be very relaxing. Stargazing is a way to get outside at night. Some people build their own telescopes and gather on hillsides to watch a light show. Looking at the huge universe lets them unwind from their daily cares.

Answer the questions below.

1. What is the paragraph mostly about? _____

2. Besides gardening, what two other hobbies are mentioned?_____

   _____

3. How are the three hobbies alike? Give at least two ways that they resemble one another. _____

   _____

4. How do the hobbies mentioned affect people? _____

   _____

5. What do the supporting details of the paragraph tell the reader about the main idea? _____

6. Sometimes the title can give us a clue about the main idea. What would be a good title for this paragraph? _____

   _____

Say What You Mean

Authors do not always come right out and say what they mean. When that is the case, readers have to use clues from the paragraph to figure out the **main idea.** Read the following paragraph.

Have you ever waited for a new toy to come out, only to find that the store sold out of it before you could buy it? Companies sometimes put out a small number of a new item. They know that people will be so eager to get the toy that they will pay higher prices. Gold is hard to find, as well as beautiful, and it is the most valuable metal on Earth. Scientists have figured out how to make oysters create pearls, but these cultured pearls are not as valuable as natural pearls. Pearls that are created naturally are harder to find and are worth more money than the ones that are helped along by science.

Choose the topic sentence that best states the main idea of the paragraph. Circle the letter of the correct answer.

a. The easier it is to find something, the more expensive it will be.

b. Something that is rare is seen as more valuable.

c. Companies should make a bigger supply of new toys.

Now, write the topic sentence in the center. Using your own words, list the details from the paragraph that support this topic sentence.

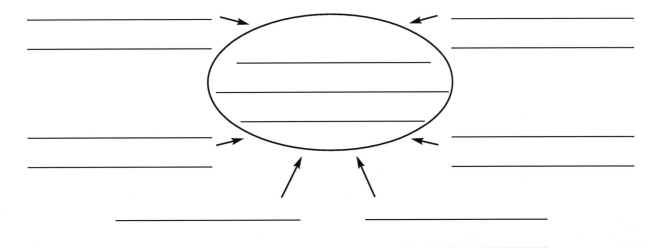

The Big Idea

Read the following essay. Underline the **main idea** in each paragraph. Then try to find the Big Idea—the main idea for the whole essay. Finally, give the essay a title.

Title: _____

Studies have shown that listening to classical music can improve math skills. This so-called "Mozart effect" is even more noticeable when people make music rather than merely listen to it. Preschool students who have had piano lessons are better at taking math tests than those with no musical instruction. Older children who have had some music lessons are better at recognizing patterns in numbers and objects. They also learn fractions more quickly and easily. These studies have led scientists to believe that there is a link between music skills and math skills. But making music has even more benefits!

People who learn to play a musical instrument learn a lot more than how to play notes. It is hard work to play an instrument. You have to develop the habit of practicing every day. You have to practice even when you don't feel like it. The reward for this effort is the thrill of making music. Other rewards include increased self-discipline and confidence in one's abilities. One can learn lessons about teamwork from playing in a band. These are great lessons to learn, but music can also help people increase their brainpower!

Even if a person does not show a lot of musical talent, learning to play an instrument is still valuable. Besides the rewards already mentioned, music helps people become more creative. It is also a great way to relieve stress. Adults who study musical instruments have better memories. Finally, learning a musical instrument can make people into lifelong music lovers. They will have a greater appreciation for all types of music.

The Big Idea: _____

Pizza or Ice Cream?

Good readers are able to identify the important facts and **details** in a paragraph. They are able to put them into their own words. That way, they are able to remember and better understand what they are reading.

Read the following paragraph. Then write the main idea and details below, using your own words.

End-of-School Party, by Randy

I think we should have pizza instead of ice cream on the last day of school. Pizza is the most popular food in our class. It is not as messy as ice cream. It is easy to serve because you don't need forks, spoons, or bowls, just paper plates. Pizza is also a healthier food choice than ice cream. That is why I vote for pizza for our end-of-school party!

---

1. **Main Idea**

   _____

2. **Details**

   _____

   _____

Sarah wants ice cream for the party. Write a main idea for her paragraph and three details that would support her topic sentence.

3. **Main Idea**

   _____

4. **Details**

   _____

   _____

Allergy Season

For each **main idea,** circle the letter of the **detail** sentence that best supports it.

1. Many people suffer from allergies.

   a. An allergy is a sensitivity to normally harmless substances.

   b. Suffering can be caused by hunger.

2. An allergic response is caused by the immune system.

   a. The immune system is like the body's police officer.

   b. Many allergies are hereditary.

3. Seasonal allergies occur in the spring, summer, or fall.

   a. Food allergies can be life-threatening.

   b. Seasonal allergies can last until winter brings the first frost.

4. Some people have food allergies.

   a. Strawberries, wheat, and peanuts are foods that often cause allergic reactions.

   b. Seasonal allergies can trigger asthma in some people.

5. Different allergies have different symptoms.

   a. Sneezing, coughing, runny nose, and itchy eyes are signs of seasonal allergies.

   b. People should avoid foods to which they are allergic.

6. Allergy treatments can help people live more comfortably.

   a. Some people are allergic to perfumes.

   b. Some medications can help reduce allergic symptoms.

For the Birds

Look at the title and the topic sentence given below. These give the **main idea** of a paragraph.

> ### Birds, Bills, and Beaks
> Instead of forks, knives, or spoons, birds have bills or beaks that are especially adapted to the kind of food they eat.

Write **Y** for detail sentences that support the main idea. Write **N** for detail sentences that do not support the main idea.

1. ___ Hummingbird tongues are actually hollow tubes for sucking nectar from flowers.

2. ___ Seed-eating birds have short, thick bills for cracking open hard seeds.

3. ___ Eagles and hawks have sharp, hooked beaks for catching and eating small animals.

4. ___ Ducks have webbed feet that they can use like paddles.

5. ___ Broad bills allow diving birds to scoop up food from the bottom of rivers and lakes.

6. ___ All birds use their bills or beaks for turning their eggs.

7. ___ There are over 9,000 species of birds.

8. ___ Woodpeckers have strong, pointed bills that let them find insects inside trees.

9. ___ A woodpecker's bill hits a tree at a rate of 13 miles per hour!

10. ___ The chickadee is the state bird of both Maine and Massachusetts.

Main Idea Ferry

In a well-written paragraph, all of the **details** point to or support the **main idea.** As you read the following paragraph, look for the main idea.

Riding the Ferry

A ferry is a special kind of boat. It can carry cars as well as people! If you want to cross a river and there is no bridge available, you might be able to take a ferry. The ferry is built so that cars can drive right onto the bottom deck. People can stay in their cars or get out and walk around. Sometimes there is a snack bar on the ferry. When the ferry docks on the other side, the front gate of the ferry opens and the cars drive right off. Ferries usually go back and forth across the same body of water, carrying cars from one side to the other. Ferries travel on the ocean as well as on rivers and large lakes.

Underline the main idea in the paragraph above and write it in the circle below. All the details in the paragraph should support this idea. Find four details from the paragraph that support the main idea. Underline the four details, and then write them on the chart so that they are pointing to the main idea. Try to use your own words when you write the details.

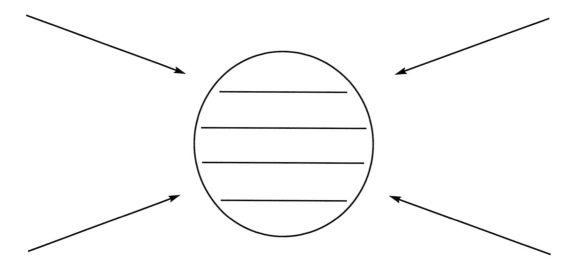

Popping Popcorn

Details are the facts or ideas that a writer uses to support the **main idea.** Some sentences in a paragraph may not be supporting details. An author might put in other small details that support a supporting detail but do not add to the main idea. When reading for information, focus on the most important details.

A Short History of Popcorn

Popcorn has a long and interesting history. Most people enjoy eating a box of popcorn at the movies, or making a batch of popcorn to enjoy at home in front of the television. In fact, most people love popcorn, but few think about what it is or how it became so popular. Popcorn has been around for over 5,000 years. Some ears of popped corn were found in a bat cave in New Mexico in 1948 and 1950 that were said to date back to 3500 B.C.E.! Some Native American groups used to put the corn right over the fire and pop it while it was still on the cob. Some would also grind popcorn into flour. Popcorn became a popular snack food in the early 1800s, but popping corn was difficult and often messy. A lot of kernels ended up in the fire. It was the invention of corn-popping devices toward the end of the century that made corn popping easier and even more popular. Popcorn was the first food to be cooked in a microwave. Today, popcorn is the number one selling snack in the world.

1. What is the main idea? _____

_____

2. List three important details that support the main idea. _____

_____

_____

_____

Notice the Details

The important **details** in a paragraph can help you figure out the **main idea.**

The Information Revolution

When you are waiting for an important package in the mail, you might start getting impatient after a day or two. You might pick up the phone and call to check on it. If you need an important document right away, you might ask someone to send a facsimile, or fax, of it. Or you could use e-mail to communicate. If you want to know what is happening in the world, you have only to turn on the radio or the television or look on the Internet. If you need to talk to relatives in another state, you can pick up the telephone. If they are not at home, you can try their cell phone number. We have so many ways of getting and receiving information that it is hard to imagine a time when people had very little means of communication.

Answer the following by circling the letter of the correct answer.

1. This paragraph lists examples of
   a. different uses of the telephone.
   b. people's lack of patience.
   c. ways of receiving information.
   d. early ways of communication.

2. When there is more than one paragraph about a topic, a transition sentence may link the paragraphs. Based on this, the next paragraph may be about
   a. telephones.
   b. earlier forms of communication.
   c. package delivery.
   d. using the Internet.

3. What is the main idea?
   a. Communication is important.
   b. Today, we have many fast and easy ways of communicating.
   c. Cell phones are important.
   d. Television is more important than radio for getting information.

Painting Details

Read the paragraph about famous painter Vincent Van Gogh and look at the underlined main idea. Put a checkmark (✔) next to the details that support the main idea.

Vincent Van Gogh

<u>Although Vincent Van Gogh had a short, unhappy life, he still produced valuable works of great art.</u> Van Gogh was a Dutch painter who lived in France. He was born on March 30, 1853 in Groot Zundert, The Netherlands. He failed at several careers before turning to painting. He was nearly always poor. Van Gogh also had a history of physical problems during his life which were due in part to his poverty and the fact that he was frequently malnourished. Van Gogh was influenced by the Impressionist painters who used a lot of light and bright colors in their paintings. While living in the south of France, he painted some beautiful pictures of flowers, including one called <u>Sunflowers</u> and another called <u>Irises</u>. His painting, <u>Irises</u>, sold for over $53 million in 1987. Van Gogh soon went beyond impressionism to a kind of expressionism, putting a lot of inner emotion into his work. <u>Starry Night</u>, painted just before his death in 1890, is the most famous work from this period. Van Gogh's paintings now sell for millions of dollars, but he sold very few paintings during his lifetime.

_____ 1. Van Gogh was a Dutch painter who lived in France.

_____ 2. He was born on March 30, 1853 in Groot Zundert, The Netherlands.

_____ 3. He failed at several careers before turning to painting.

_____ 4. Van Gogh had physical problems during his life that were due in part to his poverty and malnourishment.

_____ 5. Van Gogh was influenced by the Impressionist painters.

_____ 6. <u>Starry Night</u> is the most famous work from his expressionist period.

_____ 7. Van Gogh's paintings now sell for millions of dollars, but he sold very few paintings during his lifetime.

A Whale of a Tale

The class is doing a group project on whales. Each pair of students needs to find information on an assigned subtopic. Marika and Tim are looking for facts about their topic, the humpback whale. Tim found the following article in a nature magazine. Read the article, and underline **details** that Tim and Marika can use for their report.

Whale Migration

You probably have observed birds flying south for the winter. You probably know that this type of behavior is called *migration*. But did you know that whales also migrate? Scientists think that whales migrate for many different reasons, but the main reason is probably to find food. Gray whales make the longest migratory journeys, traveling from southern breeding grounds near Mexico up to Alaska for feeding, a round-trip of over 10,000 miles. Humpback whales travel nearly as far, from Alaska to Hawaii, a round-trip journey of about 6,000 miles. Other whales migrate, but not to such great distances.

---

1. What is the paragraph about?

   _____

   _____

2. What does the paragraph say about humpback whales?

   _____

   _____

3. Rewrite the information about humpback whales into a sentence that Marika and Tim can use in their report.

   _____

   _____

Daily Skill-Builders Reading 4–5
walch.com © 2004 Walch Publishing

Bear Necessities

Carlos has collected a lot of facts and **details** about bears from different sources. He is going to write three paragraphs about bears, so he has three topic sentences. Help Carlos figure out where each detail belongs. After each detail below, write the letter of the correct topic sentence on the line. If the detail doesn't fit with any of the topic sentences, write **N.**

Topic Sentences
a. Bears eat a lot of different kinds of food.
b. Bears are normally peaceful but can be dangerous.
c. Bears usually sleep during the winter.

Details	Topic Sentence

Source—Encyclopedia
1. Bears have no enemies except other bears and humans. _____
2. Bears like fish. _____
3. Bears eat fruits and berries. _____
4. Bears can be dangerous to humans. _____
5. Bears sometimes walk around on mild winter days. _____

Source—Newspaper article
6. A bear attacked some hikers in Colorado. _____
7. Many new homes have been built near bear habitats. _____
8. Bears do not fear humans. _____
9. Black bears look for food around campsites and cabins. _____
10. During hibernation, bears experience a drop in heart rate. _____

Source—Internet
11. Bears hunt mice and squirrels. _____
12. Bears live alone and never roam in a pack. _____
13. Bears love honey and will tear open beehives to get it. _____
14. Polar bears are good swimmers. _____
15. Bears can have quick tempers. _____

Marvelous Mushrooms

Read the paragraphs about mushrooms. Look for important **details.**

Mushrooms

Scientists used to classify mushrooms as plants, but now they are given their own kingdom alongside the plant and animal kingdoms. They are called *fungi*. Fungi might seem to be plants, but they do not need light to grow and they do not produce chlorophyll. Mushrooms feed off dead and decomposing matter and are often found growing on old tree stumps or logs. We only see the fruit of the mushroom. Its body actually exists underground and can spread over large areas. The largest known living organism is actually a honey mushroom. It has been known to spread and cover almost three and a half square miles, and is still growing!

A lot of people enjoy eating mushrooms. They are used in many fancy recipes, but taste good on a pizza as well. However, many people think that mushrooms have no nutritional value. They think mushrooms aren't good for you, because they are not green. Mushrooms actually have more potassium than bananas and also provide other essential nutrients, such as selenium and copper. Potassium is important for maintaining a normal heart rhythm, selenium helps boost the human immune system, and copper is needed to produce red blood cells. In addition, mushrooms contain B-complex vitamins that help the body get energy from food. So, mushrooms taste good and are good for you, too!

List two important details from each paragraph.

1. **Paragraph 1 Details:** _____

   _____

2. **Paragraph 2 Details:** _____

   _____

3. On the back of this paper, write the main idea of each paragraph. Do the details you listed above support your main ideas?

Picture Perfect

A **conclusion** is a reasoned judgment. When you look at a picture, you draw conclusions based on what you see happening in the picture. Write a sentence below each picture, telling what is happening. Give evidence from the picture to support the conclusion you have drawn.

1.

_____

_____

_____

2.

_____

_____

_____

3.

_____

_____

_____

4.

_____

_____

_____

Guessing Games

When you make a guess about something based on clues or facts, you are making an **inference.**

> **Example:** A man opens up his umbrella as he leaves the building.
> (*We can infer that it must be raining outside.*)

Answer the questions below by making inferences.

1. John is clearing dishes from the table. There is a crash and the sound of breaking glass.
   What happened? _____

2. The bell rings, and children rush out of the school. There are school buses waiting.
   What time of day is it? _____

3. Christina wants to buy three candy bars. When she counts out her money to pay, she puts one candy bar back on the shelf.
   Why did Christina put a candy bar back on the shelf? _____
   _____

4. Mr. Juarez is cutting down some bushes. Suddenly, he runs across the yard with a swarm of bees following him.
   Why were the bees chasing Mr. Juarez? _____
   _____

5. Hansel and Gretel left a trail of bread crumbs when they went into the forest. Some birds were watching them. When the children tried to follow the trail back out of the forest, the bread crumbs were gone.
   What happened to the bread crumbs? _____

6. Luke goes out for a bike ride. He comes back with a comic book, a can of soda, and a box of candy.
   Where did Luke go on his bike? _____

Take a Guess

Sometimes the author does not tell you every fact. Good readers make guesses **(inferences)** based on what they know and what the author says. Read the situations below, and then answer the questions that follow.

A woman, wearing a uniform, parks her truck at the side of the road. She gets out, carrying a canvas bag. She goes to every house on the street. When she returns, her canvas bag is empty. She drives to the next street and repeats the process.

1. Who is the woman? _____

2. What is she doing? _____

Fiona has two little sisters, Betty and Brenda. They are the same age and look exactly alike. Fiona cannot tell them apart unless they wear different clothes.

3. What can we infer about Betty and Brenda?_____

4. Is Fiona the oldest of the three? How do you know?_____

_____

It is a hot, sunny morning. The McDonald family is loading their car with a picnic basket, a cooler, and a large, striped umbrella. They have big towels and blankets, folding chairs, and an inflatable ball. One bag is filled with plastic pails and shovels.

5. What time of year is it? _____

6. Where are the McDonalds going? _____

"What's for dinner?" Sam asked his mom.
"We'll see when your father and brother get home," his mother replied.
"Oh, no, not fish again!" complained Sam. "I'm sick of fish!"

7. Where did Sam's father and brother go? _____

8. Why is Sam sick of fish?

_____

Ugly Duckling or Swan?

Read the following paragraph. As you read, think about what you can **infer** from the paragraph. Then answer the questions below.

Do you know the story of "The Ugly Duckling"? A mother duck hatches her eggs, but one of her ducklings is different from the rest. He is skinny, scrawny, and ugly. The mother duckling is ashamed of him. The other ducklings avoid him. The other farm animals laugh at him. The poor ugly duckling is sad and lonely. Then it turns out that he is not a duck at all, but a swan. He grows up to be beautiful and graceful. This story was written by a Danish writer of fairy tales, named Hans Christian Andersen. He was a skinny, scrawny, unattractive boy who was often sickly. He did not have many friends, as the other children made fun of him. When he grew up, he had trouble figuring out what to do with his life. Finally, he started writing stories and became famous and popular.

1. What two ideas are told in the paragraph?

   _____

   _____

2. Where do you think Hans Christian Andersen got the idea for his story, "The Ugly Duckling"? What can you infer from the paragraph?

   _____

   _____

   _____

   _____

Jump to Conclusions

We make **inferences** every day, whether we know it or not. When you make a guess about something based on clues or facts, you are making an inference. We base our inferences on what we know from our own experiences.

> **Example:** You get to the bus stop. No one is there. Usually at 3 o'clock, there are twenty people at the stop. You look at your watch. It says 3 o'clock. You might infer that you missed the bus because your watch is slow.

Make inferences about the following situations.

1. If you come home from school and the door is locked, the car is gone, and your cat is sitting on the front porch, you might infer that _____

    _____

2. If your cat is staring with great concentration at the sofa and doesn't come when called for dinner, you might infer that _____

    _____

3. If your brother comes out of the kitchen eating a cookie, and you go into the kitchen and find an empty cookie box on the counter, you might infer that _____

4. If your mother comes into the living room and finds cookie crumbs all over the floor, she might infer that _____

    _____

5. If your brother sits down with your mom and your mom looks angry, he might infer that _____

    _____

Using What We Know

We make **inferences** all the time by using clues that we pick up when reading stories. We use clues from what we already know, our **prior knowledge.** Details from the story or information we know that supports a conclusion is called **evidence.** Read the story. Then complete the chart. Write the evidence that supports each conclusion given.

The Story of Goldilocks and the Three Bears

Once upon a time, there were three bears—Papa Bear, Mama Bear, and Baby Bear. They lived together in a snug, little cottage, where they each had a special bowl for porridge, a special chair to sit in, and a special bed to sleep in. One day, a little girl named Goldilocks was walking through the woods and found a cottage. She was tired, so she knocked on the door to see if someone could help her. When no one answered, she went inside. There were three bowls of porridge on the table. One was hot, one was cold, and one was just right. Then she sat in the three chairs. Two were too big, but one was just right. Then she went upstairs and saw the beds. One was too hard, one was too soft, and one was just right. Goldilocks soon fell asleep but was awakened by the sound of the Bears coming home. Goldilocks jumped out of bed and ran all the way home.

Conclusion	Evidence
Goldilocks was hungry and tired when she arrived at the cottage, so she ate the porridge and took a nap.	**1.**
Goldilocks was afraid when she heard the sounds of the Bears coming home.	**2.**
The story of Goldilocks and the Three Bears is a fantasy or make-believe story.	**3.**

The New Neighbors

Read the following story, and then answer the questions below. As you read, look for **inferences** made by the characters in the story.

When Sally got home from school, she saw her mother's purse and keys on the front hall table. "Hi, Mom, sorry I'm late!" she called.

"That's okay," her mother replied. She looked at Sally's muddy shoes. "Did you have soccer practice?"

"Yes, they didn't want to call it off, because we have a big game on Saturday." Sally sniffed the air, "Have you been baking cookies?"

"Yes, but they're not for us. I saw a moving van in the driveway of the empty house next door."

"Wow!" Sally was excited. "I see some toys. They must have kids!"

"Yes," her mother agreed, "I think they must be younger than you, though, because they put up a swing set in the back."

"Oh, too bad." Sally thought a minute, then brightened. "They might need a babysitter, right?"

1. Sally infers that her mother is home. Why? _____

_____

2. Sally's mother infers that Sally had soccer practice. Why? _____

_____

3. Why does Sally infer that her mother has been baking? _____

_____

4. Her mother infers something about the new next-door neighbors. Why?

_____

5. What does Sally infer about the new neighbors? _____

_____

6. Now read the story again. Write two things you can infer about Sally.

_____

_____

Supposing Scientists

Making **inferences** is an important skill for scientists. For example, *paleontologists*, the scientists who study fossils, must piece together bits of evidence to arrive at their conclusions. Read the following paragraph and answer the questions below.

Were Some Dinosaurs Poisonous?

Dinosaurs have never been thought to be poisonous. Recently, however, scientists discovered a dinosaur tooth in Mexico. This tooth has a certain groove that is similar to a groove found in the fangs of some poisonous snakes, such as cobras, as well as some poisonous lizards, such as the gila monster. When biting an enemy, the grooved tooth allows the poison to flow into the bite.

---

1. What might scientists conclude from this new information?

   _____

   _____

2. What prior knowledge would they use to support this conclusion?

   _____

   _____

3. What would happen if scientists discovered a grooved tooth in a non-poisonous animal? How might they have to modify their theories?

   _____

   _____

   _____

Dinosaur Conclusions

Scientists **infer** from evidence and draw **conclusions** all the time. For instance, everything we know about dinosaurs comes from scientists who study fossils and draw conclusions about what dinosaurs were like. Sometimes, when new information is discovered, these conclusions are changed. Help scientists draw conclusions in the following instances.

1. In 1923, scientists found a new type of dinosaur skeleton on a nest of eggs in Mongolia. The new dinosaur was a predator, or meat-eater, with sharp claws, and the eggs looked like those of a plant-eating dinosaur named Protoceratops commonly found in that area. The scientists named the new dinosaur Oviraptor, which means "egg-stealer." What two pieces of evidence did the scientists have, and what did they infer from the evidence?

    _____

    _____

    _____

    _____

2. More recently, a new dinosaur egg was discovered in Mongolia. This egg looked like the eggs that were discovered in 1923 and thought to be Protoceratops. However, this egg contained a tiny skeleton, not of a Protoceratops, but of an Oviraptor! What new conclusions do you think the scientists could infer from this information?

    _____

    _____

    _____

    _____

Ad Smart

The people who write advertisements want consumers to make **inferences** about their products. What do you think the following ads are hoping we will infer? What product are they trying to sell?

1. A boy is standing by himself looking lonely. Another boy comes by and gives him a bottle of "Cool Cola." The next scene shows the boy looking happy, surrounded by a crowd of friends.

_____

_____

_____

_____

2. A magazine shows a computer screen with Smart Stuff Software displayed. A smiling boy is showing a report card with all A's to his mother, who is also smiling.

A+

_____

_____

_____

_____

3. A happy family is sitting together on a sofa. They are watching television and laughing together. They have a big bowl of Happy Times Popcorn in front of them.

POP CORN

_____

_____

_____

_____

4. A man feeds his dog Good Puppy dog food, and the dog is shown running happily through the fields.

_____

_____

_____

_____

Daily Skill·Builders Reading 4–5
walch.com © 2004 Walch Publishing

What Happens Next?

Look at the pictures and make a **prediction** about what might happen next. Use clues from the picture to explain why you made your prediction. The first one has been done for you.

1.

Prediction: ___The girl is going to___

___school.___

Why? ___She is getting on the___

___school bus.___

2.

Prediction: _____

_____

Why? _____

_____

3.

Prediction: _____

_____

Why? _____

_____

4.

Prediction: _____

_____

Why? _____

_____

Predicting Patterns

We learn to predict **outcomes** (what will happen) from patterns. Read the following patterns and answer the questions.

1. If you were watching a mother duck waddle out of the barn with four white ducklings behind her, what color would you predict the fifth duckling to be?

   _____

2. If you were reading a picture book to your baby sister and the first page had a red circle, the second page a red square, the third page a blue circle, what would you predict the fourth page to be?

   _____

3. Suppose your neighbor washes his car every Saturday, unless it rains. If Saturday is a sunny day, what would you guess your neighbor might do?

   _____

4. If your dad always watches the football games on television on Sunday afternoons in the fall, where would you expect him to be on a Sunday in October?

   _____

5. Now write your own pattern below.

   _____

   _____

   _____

Daily Skill-Builders Reading 4–5
walch.com © 2004 Walch Publishing

Title Clues

On a visit to the library, John and Mary looked at books. John likes fantasy and mystery books. Mary likes history, science, and fact books. Write John or Mary next to each title, based on what you predict the book might be about.

1. True Stories from Pioneer Days _____

2. Neil Armstrong, First Man on the Moon _____

3. The Case of the Missing Shoe _____

4. All About Dogs _____

5. All About Rocks _____

6. The Singing Hippo _____

7. The Monster of the Deep _____

8. George Washington, Father of our Country _____

9. The Mystery of the Missing Monkey _____

10. True Horse Stories _____

Tippy Canoe

Read the following paragraph, and **predict** what will happen next.

Sandy and Bill are at summer camp. There is a lesson in water safety. They will be trying out a canoe. "Never stand up in a canoe," cautions the camp counselor. "Canoes are very light and unstable. You can easily tip a canoe over." Sandy and Bill aren't listening. They are watching an ant climb over Sandy's sneaker. Every time it climbs over, Sandy puts his sneaker in front of the ant and it climbs over again. When it is time to get in the canoe, they have to be reminded to wear life jackets. "Weren't you listening to the counselor?" asks Lin. "You have to wear a life jacket when you paddle a canoe."

Answer the questions below.

1. The counselor tells the children never to stand up in a canoe. We can infer from the paragraph that he told them something else. What else do you think the counselor said, and why do you think that?

   _____

   _____

2. What do you think might happen once Bill and Sandy get in the canoe?

   _____

   _____

3. Why do you think that? _____

   _____

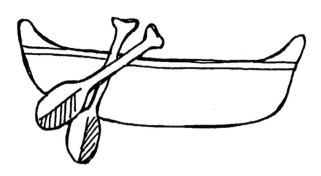

Predicting the Future

Sometimes we make **inferences** when we make **predictions** about what might happen next. Predictions are often based on **prior knowledge,** that is, what we have already learned through our experiences. Answer the questions below.

1. A little boy is eating a bowl of ice cream at a pool party on a sunny day. He puts his ice cream down and plays in the sandbox for awhile. What do you think happens to the ice cream?

_____

What prior knowledge do you have about ice cream that helped you make this prediction?

_____

2. A little girl is holding a kitten. A big dog barks at the kitten and scares the little girl. What do you think happens next?

_____

What do you know about cats and dogs that supports your prediction?

_____

3. Drivers have to be alert for pedestrians or children playing in the road at all times. Adults know that children play with balls. If a ball rolls into the street, what do you think the driver of a car would do?

_____

What prior knowledge does the driver have that would make him or her react this way?

_____

Happy Endings

We make **predictions** based on what we expect to happen. Sometimes our predictions are correct, and sometimes they are not. Answer the questions below.

Once upon a time, there lived a King and a Queen who had no children.

1. From the first sentence, what kind of story do you predict this will be?
   - **a.** an adventure story
   - **b.** a fairy tale
   - **c.** a mystery
   - **d.** a scary story

   Why? _____

   _____

The King very much wanted a child and went to a witch who lived near his castle to ask for her help.

2. What do you think the witch will be like and why?

   _____

   _____

3. Do you think it is a good idea for the King to go to the witch? Why or why not? _____

   _____

Now, the witch was actually a very good witch, and she wanted to help the king. After working on some magic spells, she came across an orphan in the forest. The very next day, she was able to present the child to the King.

The End

4. Were you surprised by the ending to this story? Why? _____

   _____

Lemonade for Sale!

Read the following story, and make **predictions** of what may happen next. Then answer the questions below.

Meg and Millie are friends. They live near a busy park. People walk, ride bikes, and in-line skate on the path that goes behind their houses. One hot summer Saturday, they decide to set up a lemonade stand. They make two large pitchers of pink lemonade and put up a sign. They are selling pink lemonade for twenty-five cents a cup. By noon, they have made $5.00. They have to make two more pitchers of lemonade.

1. Why is Saturday a good day for Meg and Millie to set up a lemonade stand? _____

_____

2. How is the weather helping Meg and Millie sell lemonade? _____

_____

3. Do you predict that they will sell more or less lemonade in the afternoon? Why or why not? _____

_____

4. What do you think will happen if black clouds start to cover the sky?

_____

5. What do you think will happen if some other children set up a lemonade stand and charge ten cents a cup? _____

_____

Monkey Business!

Read the following paragraphs carefully, and answer the questions below. As you read, make **predictions** of what will happen next.

Three monkeys were sitting in a tree. They were bored. It was a very hot day. No breeze was blowing. Steam seemed to rise from the forest floor. "Let's go to the water hole," suggested the youngest monkey. "No!" said the oldest monkey. The oldest monkey was reading a book and was not as bored as the other two. "We promised we would stay here and wait for our mother," the middle monkey added. Looking up, the youngest monkey saw a tempting bunch of bananas just out of reach.

1. What do you think will happen next? Why? _____

_____

The youngest monkey climbed up, clung with one toe and hung by its tail. Oh, no! The bunch of bananas fell right on top of the oldest monkey's head. The youngest monkey knew it was in trouble! The oldest monkey dropped its book and started chasing the youngest monkey. "Oh, dear, oh, dear," cried the middle monkey, following its brothers. The youngest monkey was screeching! The oldest monkey was bellowing with anger! Suddenly, they all stopped. They were panting. They were dripping with sweat. There, below them, shimmering in the sunlight, looking so cool and inviting, was the water hole!

2. What do you think will happen next?_____

_____

Fire!

Read the following paragraphs, and make **predictions** of what will happen next. Then answer the questions below.

> Sometimes wildfires burn out of control. Recently a wildfire in Arizona burned over 8,000 acres and destroyed more than 250 homes. People were evacuated to safe places as the fire spread. In the previous year, a lack of rain made the pine forest extremely dry, so the fire was very difficult to control. Strong winds were pushing the fire toward more homes and trees.

1. After a year of very little rain (called a *drought*), what do you think firefighters might predict? _____

2. What does *evacuated* mean? _____

3. What do you predict might happen if the wind dies down or changes direction? _____

> Besides the five-year drought, the forests have been weakened by bark beetles. These tiny black bugs attack unhealthy trees. A healthy tree can usually produce enough sap to smother the beetles, but a tree that has been suffering from drought does not have the strength to resist the beetles. In some parts of the West, once healthy, green forests are now brown.

4. Why are the forests brown? _____

5. If you know that dead trees burn faster than green, living trees, what do you predict might happen if a fire gets started in a dry, partly dead forest?

_____

Flood!

Read the following paragraphs, and make **predictions** of what will happen next. Then answer the questions below.

> One spring, a week of heavy rainfall caused the waters of Lake Manatee in Florida to rise five feet above normal. Since people like to build houses near water, they are sometimes in danger when the water level rises. During flood warnings, people are moved to higher ground; this is called *evacuation*. Lake Manatee has special dams that help officials control water levels. If the lake gets too high, they can release some of the water out of the lake by opening the flood gates.

1. What do you predict the officials will do when they realize more rain is on the way? _____

   _____

> This time, however, one of the floodgates on Lake Manatee was broken! Officials were unable to drain the lake fast enough. Many people have homes on the shore of Lake Manatee.

2. What do you predict officials will do next? _____

   _____

> At Lake Manatee, they used divers and cranes to get the floodgates opened. The lake level began dropping quickly and was soon below normal. People were allowed to return to their homes and begin cleaning up the damage.

3. What sort of damage do you think a flood might cause? Think what might happen if your house filled with water and then it drained out again. _____

   _____

   _____

Why Does It Happen?

What makes something happen is called a **cause.** What happens is the **effect.**

> **Example:** If you exercise each day, you will stay fit.
> What happened? You stay fit. **(effect)**
> Why? You exercised each day. **(cause)**

Answer the following by writing a cause or an effect on the line provided.

What is the **cause?**

1. If you _____, you will get an A on the test.

2. If you _____, you will spoil your appetite for dinner.

3. If you _____, you will get your allowance.

4. If you _____, you will win the race.

5. If you _____, you will get well.

What is the **effect?**

6. If you leave ice cream out in the sun, _____

7. If you forget to water your plants, _____

8. If you don't brush your teeth, _____

9. If you run on icy steps, _____

10. If you don't listen in class, _____

Tell Me Why

Understanding **cause and effect** helps you understand what you are reading. Create a cause and effect statement for each situation below.

1. "I'm sorry I am late! I was stuck in a traffic jam!" said Mrs. Hasan. Mrs. Hasan was late because _____

_____

2. "I can't go to the mall. I have too much homework." Jane complained. Jane cannot go to the mall because _____

_____

3. "It's all your fault, Brian! I would have made the team if you hadn't lost my baseball glove!" Timmy accused. Timmy thinks he did not make the team because _____

_____

4. "It's raining. Now, we have to stay inside for recess," the teacher explained. The class has to stay in for recess because _____

_____

5. "It's been raining for a week! The river might flood," the newsman reported. The river might flood because _____

_____

6. "I don't want to go swimming. The water is too cold," said Chrissy. Chrissy doesn't want to go swimming because _____

_____

Daily Skill-Builders Reading 4–5
walch.com © 2004 Walch Publishing

Red Letter Words

Cause and effect helps us make sense of what we read. Some words that signal a cause and effect relationship are as follows:

if . . . then	**If** you eat too much candy, **then** you will feel sick.
because	He felt sad **because** his friend did not call or write.
since	**Since** the sun was shining, they went to the beach.
so	He dropped the glass, **so** it broke.
therefore	They hate the beach; **therefore,** they never go.
consequently	She never studies; **consequently,** her grades are bad.
as a result	**As a result** of John's studying, he got an A in math.
due to	**Due to** the bad weather, the class stayed in for recess.
because of	I am carrying an umbrella **because of** the weather forecast.

Read the following paragraph, and underline the words that signal a cause and effect relationship.

Winston wished he could go to his friend's pool party. But, because Winston did not know how to swim, his mother would not let him go. Winston had tried swimming lessons in the past but did not like the instructor. Consequently, he refused to go back to her class. His mother said, "If you wear a life jacket the whole time, then you can go to the party." Winston did not want to wear a life jacket because everyone would know he couldn't swim. When the invitation to the party came in the mail, Winston left it unopened on the table. As a result, the envelope was lying on the table when his mother got home. "Listen, Winston," she said, reading aloud, "Due to the fact that most of the children who were invited don't know how to swim, we are having a 'learn to swim' party. Our older daughter is a swim instructor. Because of this, we felt that she could teach the children at the pool party how to swim." This was good news! Winston could go to the party and learn to swim at the same time.

Proverbs

A proverb is a short, witty saying that usually teaches a lesson. Maybe you have heard some of the following proverbs. Think about what lessons they are teaching and rewrite them as **cause and effect** sentences.

1. Waste not, want not.

   If _____ ,

   then _____

2. Early to bed, early to rise, makes a man healthy, wealthy, and wise.

   If _____ ,

   then _____

3. A penny saved is a penny earned.

   If _____ ,

   then _____

4. Haste makes waste.

   If _____ ,

   then _____

5. Practice makes perfect.

   If _____ ,

   then _____

6. Where there's a will, there's a way.

   If _____ ,

   then _____

7. Money can't buy happiness.

   If _____ ,

   then _____

Daily Skill-Builders Reading 4–5
walch.com © 2004 Walch Publishing

Family Feuds

Read the following stories, and look for **cause and effect** in each. Then answer the questions that follow each story.

> "Shhh, you'll wake up the baby," said Melissa when her brother came running into the house. Sure enough, the baby woke up and started to cry. "Oh, sorry," said Jared, stopping in his tracks and starting to tiptoe. But it was too late. "You'll have to play with him," said Melissa, "because I have to finish making dinner."

1. Why did the baby wake up (cause)? _____

_____

2. What happened to Jared (effect)? _____

_____

> Mrs. Jones called the family together. She was holding a paper and was frowning. "This is it!" she cried. "Look at this electric bill—it is higher than ever! We all need to be more careful about leaving the lights on all the time." Mrs. Jones's children looked guilty. They knew they often forgot to turn the lights off. Mrs. Jones had a plan. "From now on, whoever leaves a light on when they are not in a room will have to put a quarter in this jar." She held up a jar.

3. Why was the electric bill so high (cause)? _____

_____

4. What did Mr. Jones decide to do (effect)? _____

_____

Because, Because, Because

Read the following story, and then answer the questions.

The Wonderful Wizard

In the movie <u>The Wizard of Oz</u>, Dorothy and her friends sing about going to see the wonderful wizard of Oz because of the wonderful things he does. In the story, Dorothy wants to go home to Kansas. She misses her family. Because the Wizard is so wonderful, she wants to ask him for help. She makes friends with a Scarecrow, who asks to join her on her journey. He wants to ask the Wizard for a brain. Next, they meet the Tinman; after they oil his joints so he can move and talk again, he also has a wish. He wishes for a heart, so he goes with them to ask the Wizard for one. Finally, the Cowardly Lion joins their quest, so he can ask for the gift of courage.

---

1. Why does Dorothy need to see the Wizard? _____

   _____

2. Why does the Scarecrow go to see the Wizard? _____

   _____

3. Why does the Tinman go to see the Wizard? _____

   _____

4. Why does the Lion go to see the Wizard? _____

   _____

A Cause-Effect Move

Read the following paragraph, and look for **cause and effect** in the story. Then answer the questions below.

One day, Muriel overheard her mother talking on the telephone. "Oh," she said, "How I wish we had never moved from our old town. The children seem miserable. I know they miss their friends. They write letters and talk on the phone, but I know that they miss going to the park with them. They are having a difficult time meeting new friends. They are sometimes uncomfortable being the new students in class. I feel terrible that they had to leave their dog behind and find it another home. I know they miss Harvey very much! I see a difference in their behavior. They are both quiet and sad. Their school grades are not as high as usual. Oh, I wish we had stayed where we were!"

1. Muriel's mother sees that her children are miserable. List a cause for their sorrow. _____

   _____

2. Now, list some of the effects. What changes does the mother see in her children since they moved? _____

   _____

   _____

   _____

   _____

How Hurricanes Happen

Read the following paragraphs, and look for **causes** of hurricanes.

Hurricanes start out as thunderstorms off the west coast of Africa. They gather strength from the warm ocean waters and move across the Atlantic Ocean. Warm air is drawn up from the surface of the water. This air condenses to form storm clouds. This causes the cooler air in the atmosphere to warm up and rise, which then draws more warm air from the ocean. This cycle creates the strong counterclockwise winds of the hurricane. The winds swirl around a central calm spot, called an *eye*.

Another factor in the formation of hurricanes is *converging winds*. Winds that are going in different directions collide and push warm air from the ocean surface. This adds to the air already rising to give strength to the hurricane.

When warm air rises into the atmosphere, it causes a low pressure system. That is, the pressure of the air pushing down on the earth is less than normal. Because of the rapidly rising warm air in a hurricane, the air pressure in the center of the storm is extremely low. Hurricanes suck air into the low pressure center, increasing the force of the winds.

List four causes of hurricanes.

1. _____

2. _____

3. _____

4. _____

Disaster Relief

Read the following paragraphs, and look for the **effects** of hurricanes.

> Hurricanes are powerful and dangerous events. They often cause death, destruction, pain, and suffering. Because hurricanes form enormous storm clouds, they bring a lot of rain with them. Once they hit land and the rain begins to fall, hurricanes can cause extensive flooding. Floods can strand or kill people and damage houses and other property. Floods can also contaminate the water supply, which can lead to illness.
>
> Huge winds make up the hurricane's pattern and can destroy trees and small buildings. Downed power lines can be a fire hazard. People need to find safe places during a hurricane so they are not trapped in a damaged building. These winds can also push huge waves toward the shore, causing more flooding, beach erosion, and damage to property.

List four effects of hurricanes.

1. _____

2. _____

3. _____

4. _____

Stephen's Island Wren

Read the following story, and underline the **cause and effect** words. Then answer the question below.

Stephen's Island is a tiny island off the coast of New Zealand. The island lies in a strait, that is, a narrow passage of water that connects two larger bodies of water. Since boats often travel through the strait, it was decided that the island needed a lighthouse. The lighthouse keeper did not want to be lonely on the tiny island, so he brought along his cat, Tibbles, in 1894.

At this time, a tiny bird lived on the island. This bird may have lived on the larger islands of New Zealand before mammals were introduced. But now the bird was confined to one small island, less than one square mile. Because islands are cut off from mainland areas where mammals live, the birds often have no natural predators. Some scientists think this is why many island birds are unable to fly—they do not have the need to escape from other animals! The little wren that lived on Stephen's Island was a flightless bird. It seemed to live in a hole and come out at twilight to scurry about the bushes eating bugs. Before 1894, scientists had never even heard of this little bird.

Then, in 1894, Tibbles came to live on the island. Since, at that time, there was no canned cat food available, cats had to find their own food. Cats are carnivores and predators, so they eat meat and hunt for their dinners. Because the little wrens could not fly away and were not used to predators, Tibbles had no problem catching them for his dinner. As a result of Tibbles' hunting success, the Stephen's Island Wren became extinct.

What are three causes for the extinction of the Stephen's Island wrens?

1. _____

2. _____

3. _____

Fact or Opinion?

A **fact** is something that is true and can be proved. An **opinion** is what someone _thinks_ may or may not be true. Look at the pictures below. Write **F** for **fact** or **O** for **opinion** next to each statement.

1.

___ This is a frog.

___ Frogs are beautiful.

2.

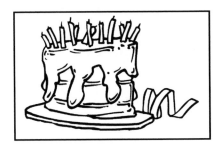

___ This is a cake.

___ This cake tastes great!

3.

___ Flowers are boring.

___ Flowers need water.

4.

___ Bats eat mosquitoes.

___ Bats are scary.

5.

___ This dog is mean.

___ Dogs should not be tied up.

6.

___ Birds have feathers.

___ Feathers are lucky.

Finish the Facts

Complete each sentence to make it a **fact** (something that is true and can be proved). Be sure to use end punctuation where needed.

1. The earth is a _____

2. Apples are a kind of _____

3. Flowers grow in the _____

4. Snow falls in the _____

5. One plus one equals _____

6. Ice cream is _____

7. Fish have _____ to breathe.

8. Whales live in the _____

9. The sun is _____

10. Airplanes have _____

11. Cars use _____ as fuel.

12. People have _____ fingers.

13. Birds build _____ in the spring.

14. Birds _____ in the air.

Opinions, Please

Opinions are important, too! Your opinions are what help make you different from others. When it comes to opinions, there are no right or wrong answers. Now write an opinion about each of the following pictures.

1.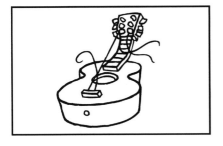

_____

_____

2.

_____

_____

3.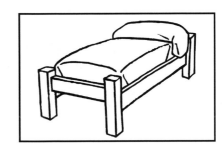

_____

_____

4.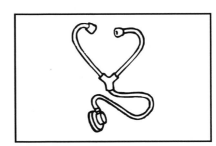

_____

_____

5.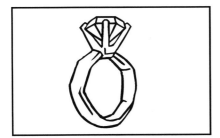

_____

_____

6.

_____

_____

State Your Own . . .

Write a **fact** and an **opinion** about each topic.

1. The sun (fact) _____
   (opinion) _____

2. Trees (fact) _____
   (opinion) _____

3. Winter (fact) _____
   (opinion) _____

4. Pizza (fact) _____
   (opinion) _____

5. My school (fact) _____
   (opinion) _____

6. Basketball (fact) _____
   (opinion) _____

7. George Washington (fact) _____
   (opinion) _____

8. Sharks (fact) _____
   (opinion) _____

9. Babies (fact) _____
   (opinion) _____

10. The American Revolution (fact) _____
    (opinion) _____

Daily Skill-Builders Reading 4–5
walch.com © 2004 Walch Publishing

Fact Check

A **fact** is something that is true and can be proved. An **opinion** is your own personal feeling about something. Look at the list below, and write a check mark (✔) under fact or opinion for each sentence. Be careful—just because you agree with a statement does not mean that it is a fact!

		Fact	Opinion
1.	The United States is in North America.	_____	_____
2.	Mars is the fourth planet from the sun.	_____	_____
3.	It is fun to swim in the ocean.	_____	_____
4.	Baseball is the most exciting game to watch.	_____	_____
5.	All girls like to play with dolls.	_____	_____
6.	People should be nice to one another.	_____	_____
7.	Golf is more exciting than tennis.	_____	_____
8.	Fish will die if they stay out of the water.	_____	_____
9.	Ice cream is cold.	_____	_____
10.	Ice cream is delicious.	_____	_____
11.	Some snakes are poisonous.	_____	_____
12.	Plants need water to live.	_____	_____
13.	Thomas Jefferson was our third president.	_____	_____
14.	Honey bees gather pollen from flowers.	_____	_____
15.	Cats are not friendly pets.	_____	_____

Let's Go to the Movies

Mac and Maureen are having an argument about which movie to see. They each have an **opinion.** Read their conversation. Then answer the questions below.

Maureen: "Let's go see <u>The Blob</u>. It's a monster movie."

    Mac: "Monster movies are stupid. Let's go see <u>Space Warriors</u>; it's a movie about aliens attacking the earth."

Maureen: "Movies about space are boring."

    Mac: "But my favorite actor is in it, Mel Mason."

Maureen: "But <u>The Blob</u> got four stars from the <u>Daily Review</u> newspaper."

    Mac: "They don't know what they're talking about. Besides, <u>Space Warriors</u> starts sooner. If we go to <u>The Blob</u>, we have to wait another hour."

Maureen: "Okay, but next time, I get to choose the movie."

---

1. What is Maureen's opinion of space movies? _____

    _____

2. What does Mac think about monster movies? _____

    _____

3. What fact does Maureen use to try to persuade Mac to see <u>The Blob</u>?

    _____

4. Where did Maureen find her fact? _____

    _____

5. What is Mac's opinion of <u>The Daily Review</u>? _____

    _____

6. What fact does Mac use to win the argument? _____

    _____

Research the Facts

Keisha has to write a research paper for school. A research paper can have an opinion for a topic sentence, but should be mostly made up of facts. See if you can help her by writing **F** for **fact** or **O** for **opinion** after each sentence.

Dogs

1. Dogs are useful animals. ( ) **2.** Dogs have been friends to humans for thousands of years. ( ) **3.** They are used for hunting and companionship. ( ) **4.** Some dogs, such as Seeing-Eye dogs, sheepherding dogs, or sled dogs work hard. ( ) **5.** Some dogs can help protect your home. ( ) **6.** These are called watchdogs. ( ) **7.** Dogs help around the house. ( ) **8.** They can chase squirrels away from your yard. ( ) **9.** Dogs like to bury bones. ( ) **10.** Dogs are friendly to other dogs and people, too. ( ) **11.** Dogs are cute and fun to be with. ( ) **12.** Everyone should own a dog. ( )

13. What is Keisha's topic sentence? _____

14. What facts support her topic sentence? (Find at least three facts.)

_____

_____

_____

15. Find one fact that does not support Keisha's topic sentence.

_____

A Trip to the Art Museum

People like many different kinds of art. Art critics are paid to give their opinions about art. When you visit an art museum, however, it is fun to form your own opinions about what is a meaningful or beautiful work of art. When Jake and Sarah visited the art museum, they had many different opinions about what they saw. Write **F** for **fact** or **O** for **opinion** after each of their comments.

1. "That painting is black streaks on a white background," remarked Jake. _____

2. "But, it's interesting," said Sarah. "It makes you think about why the artist painted it that way." _____

3. "It doesn't make any sense," insisted Jake. "A baby could have painted it." _____

4. Sarah consulted the museum catalog, "It was painted in 1953." _____

5. She continued to read: "The artist was Alberto Bartolo." _____

6. Jake was unimpressed. "I don't call this a work of art." _____

7. Sarah was still reading from the catalog: "Critics say that Bartolo achieved something entirely new with his black on white paintings." _____

8. Is the previous sentence a fact or an opinion? Who is Sarah quoting?

_____

_____

_____

Newspaper Facts

People read the newspaper to get **facts** about what is going on in their city, in the country, and in the world. Not everything in the newspaper, however, is a fact. Editorials, for example, express **opinions.** Read the following editorials, and underline the opinions. Then list the facts that are used to back up the opinions.

> The biggest embarrassment to our town is the state of the lake! It has been named the "most-polluted lake in the county" by the Department of Water Safety. It is no longer possible to swim in the lake. Boating is unsafe and unpleasant. Wildlife populations are disappearing. We all know the lake is in terrible shape, but it is time to do something about it. People have to be willing to pay more taxes so we can clean up the lake.

1. Facts: _____

_____

> The lake is not our most important problem. Our town has many other more urgent issues to deal with. It is unfair to expect people to pay higher taxes just to have a clean lake. A clean lake is a luxury in this day and age. Only people who like to swim care about it. There are other lakes nearby for swimming and boating. We need to just leave the lake the way it is.

2. Facts: _____

_____

3. In your opinion, which editorial is the most persuasive? Why?

_____

_____

Stamps of Approval

Read the following paragraphs, and determine the **opinions.** Then answer the questions below.

Everybody should have a hobby! Stamp collecting is a hobby that many people all over the world enjoy. Stamps are used to send mail to other towns, states, and even countries. Stamps are easy to buy and inexpensive, so anyone can get involved in this fun pastime. New stamps are issued all the time, some with colorful pictures commemorating famous people or events. In the past, the United States post office has issued stamps to remember famous civil rights leader Dr. Martin Luther King, Jr., as well as sports figures, such as baseball heroes Jackie Robinson and Babe Ruth. Poets, writers, and presidents have also been featured on postage stamps.

To get started in stamp collecting, you can buy a kit at the post office. A person who collects stamps is called a *philatelist*; stamp collecting is called *philately*. Some beginners wonder whether to collect used (called *canceled*) or unused (called *mint*) stamps. Canceled stamps are less expensive, and the cancellation marks add to the stamp's beauty. But mint stamps are a better investment.

1. There is one opinion in the first paragraph. Underline that sentence.

2. In the second paragraph, underline the two opinions that are given about which type of stamp to collect—mint or canceled.

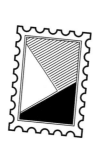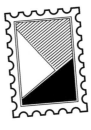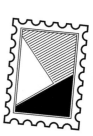

Sum It Up!

Summarizing helps us remember what we read. To summarize, use your own words and give only the most important information.

   Example: Jonathan went to the store. He rode his bike. He has a blue
   bike. It was a nice day. He bought milk and rode home.
   Summary: Jonathan rode his bike to the store to buy milk.

Read the following paragraphs and cross out what is not important. Use what is left to create a summary sentence.

---

1. Ricky has a goldfish. He keeps it in a bowl on his desk. Ricky has his own room with two windows. Ricky likes to watch his goldfish as it swims around and around in its bowl. Ricky sometimes has trouble finishing his homework.

Summary: _____

_____

_____

---

2. Cindy plays the piano. She has been playing since first grade. She likes to listen to music, too. Her brother, Phil, plays the drums. They love to make up songs to play together. Someday, they want to be in a band together.

Summary: _____

_____

_____

Summarizing Lists

Summarizing can be used to combine a list of items to one term or phrase that includes all of the items. Read each sentence, and underline the items that are listed. Then rewrite the sentence using a term or phrase instead of the underlined words.

> **Example:** I have a <u>rake</u>, a <u>shovel</u>, a <u>hoe</u>, a <u>bucket</u>, and a <u>hose</u>.
> Summary: I have some gardening tools.

1. In the junkyard they found a radiator, fender, horn, and a steering wheel.

   _____

2. It's fun to see the cows, chickens, rooster, ducks, goat, and horses.

   _____

3. I can recognize cirrus, cumulus, stratus, and thunderheads.

   _____

4. I saw an airplane, a boat, an automobile, a train, and a bicycle.

   _____

5. I heard French, Spanish, Chinese, and Khmer spoken at the festival.

   _____

6. Tonight we have cake, pie, cookies, ice cream, pudding, and gelatin.

   _____

7. This book is about fish, sharks, coral, clams, seaweed, and whales.

   _____

8. I want to learn about Washington, Jefferson, Lincoln, and Roosevelt.

   _____

Daily Skill-Builders Reading 4–5
walch.com © 2004 Walch Publishing

Summarizing Tiffany

Read the following paragraphs. As you read, look for words that can be cut out to **summarize** the story. Then answer the questions below.

> Tiffany wants to buy a special gift for her mother. She decides to earn some extra money. She washes dishes. She vacuums. She even washes the car. When she has saved enough money, she selects a beautiful rose bush at the garden store.

1. Underline all the things that Tiffany does to earn money. Now, see if you can use one word or phrase to describe how Tiffany earns money.

   _____

2. Then use your phrase to write a summary of the paragraph.

   _____

   _____

   _____

> Tiffany likes to read. She reads at night before going to bed. She reads in the morning before breakfast. She reads in the afternoon when she gets home from school. She goes to the library almost every day. The town park is next to the library. Tiffany won the school reading contest two years in a row.

3. Underline all the times that Tiffany reads. Then describe Tiffany's reading using one word or phrase.

   _____

   _____

   _____

Mary and Her Lamb

Read the following familiar nursery rhyme. Next to each verse, write a one-sentence **summary** in your own words, using only the most important information.

Mary had a little lamb,

Its fleece was white as snow,

And everywhere that Mary went

The lamb was sure to go.

1. _____

_____

_____

_____

It followed her to school one day

That was against the rule;

It made the children laugh and play

To see the lamb at school.

2. _____

_____

_____

_____

So the teacher turned him out,

But still he lingered near,

And waited patiently about

Till Mary did appear.

3. _____

_____

_____

_____

"What makes the lamb love Mary so?"

The eager children cry.

"Oh, Mary loves the lamb, you know,"

The teacher did reply.

4. _____

_____

_____

_____

Daily Skill-Builders Reading 4–5
walch.com © 2004 Walch Publishing

The Maine Idea

Good readers know how to summarize! A **summary** is a short sentence that sums up what the paragraph is about. Read the following paragraph and underline the main idea.

It is nice to visit Maine in the summer. Maine has a beautiful, rocky coastline with many quaint villages to explore. There are islands that are just a boat ride away, as well as mountains waiting to be climbed, clean and quiet lakes for swimming or boating, and wonderful people to get to know.

Look at the following summary sentences. Identify details from the paragraph that support each sentence, and write them on the lines provided.

1. Maine is beautiful. _____

_____

_____

2. There is a lot to do in Maine in the summer. _____

_____

_____

3. Which sentence in the paragraph is the best summary of the paragraph? Why? _____

_____

_____

Pandas

When creating a **summary,** you have to choose which facts are important. Some details are not important enough to include, or else they do not support the main idea. Other details repeat something that has already been said. The key to a good summary is knowing what to leave out!

Read the following paragraph, and then answer the questions below.

Pandas are only found in one small area in the mountains of China. They only eat a certain kind of plant called bamboo. The bamboo is a pretty plant. Pandas are an endangered species because people are cutting down the forests where bamboo grows. Pandas are shy creatures. If you are lucky, you might see a panda at a zoo.

1. In this paragraph, is it important that pandas eat bamboo? _____

2. In this paragraph, is it important that bamboo is a pretty plant? _____

3. Why are pandas endangered? _____

_____

4. In this paragraph, is it important that pandas are endangered? _____

5. What would be a good summary sentence for this paragraph?

_____

_____

You're Invited

Read the following paragraph and be able to **summarize** the information. Then answer the questions below.

> Jane is planning her birthday party for Saturday, May 10, at 2 P.M. She made invitations with soccer balls on the front. Jane loves soccer. She made a guest list and carefully wrote out each invitation. She invited all her friends from school and her friends from Girl Scouts and her friends who live in her neighborhood. She is planning to bake a special cake. Jane wants her twelfth birthday to be extra-special.

1. In this paragraph, is it important that Jane loves soccer? _____

2. Why does Jane think her birthday should be extra-special? _____

   _____

3. What would be a good summary sentence for the paragraph? Use only the most important information.

   _____

   _____

You Be the Judge!

Judges have to listen to people who disagree and then decide who is correct according to law. Usually there are lawyers who sum up the facts of the case for the judge.

Max and Vic are having a disagreement. Read the following dialogue, and write a short **summary** of each one's point of view.

> *Max:* I can't believe you told the teacher on us!
>
> *Vic:* But I had to tell, Max. I was the hall monitor!
>
> *Max:* But I thought we were friends!
>
> *Vic:* You disobeyed the rules. You shouldn't have been writing on the walls.
>
> *Max:* You still shouldn't tell on your friends. Now I'm going to get in trouble.
>
> *Vic:* I had to do my job.
>
> *Max:* Tattletale!
>
> *Vic:* Baby!

1. Write one sentence about what Max thinks.

   _____

   _____

2. Write one sentence about what Vic thinks.

   _____

   _____

3. Who do you think is right? What point was made that convinced you?

   _____

   _____

Movie Talk

Read the following paragraph, and circle the main idea. Then underline important details.

> Movies made from classic stories, such as <u>Peter Pan</u> or <u>Alice in Wonderland</u>, are fun to watch, but they should not replace the books. Movie directors are able to show through actions what a writer must use words to describe. Directors also must cut out many scenes so that the movie will not be too long. Often directors change endings or details to make the plot fit their own ideas. Children who never read classic works like <u>Peter Pan</u> are missing out on fantastic dialogue, characters, and beautifully described settings that are not included in the movie version. Movies should not take the place of these great books.

Now write a **summary** of the paragraph using the main idea and important details that you underlined. **Remember:** A summary should be short and should only tell the most important ideas from a piece of writing. Use your own words when writing a summary.

_____

_____

_____

_____

_____

_____

Get Your Peanuts!

Read the following paragraphs, and write a **summary** of each below.

Did you know that peanuts are not really nuts? They are part of the family of peas and beans, called legumes. Legumes have edible seeds inside pods. Most legumes grow their pods on vines or bushes, but peanuts have pods that mature underground. Peanuts are a truly unique plant.

Peanuts seem to have originated in South America. Archaeologists have dug up peanut shells at sites that are 5,000 years old. Spanish and Portuguese explorers brought the peanut back to Europe and Africa. Traders then carried the peanut to India and China. Peanut oil is still the most widely-used oil in China and other parts of Asia. During the slave trade, peanuts made the journey to North America.

Peanut butter was invented in the late 1800s as a nutritious food for senior citizens. Over time, it became popular with children in a peanut-butter and jelly sandwich. More than 500 peanuts are used to make a jar of peanut butter. About half of the peanuts grown in the United States are used in peanut butter. Peanut butter is nutritious and inexpensive, and it continues to be popular in this country.

1. Paragraph 1: _____

_____

2. Paragraph 2: _____

_____

3. Paragraph 3: _____

_____

Name that Category

A good way to remember facts is to organize them by **class** or **category.** Look at each list of items below and figure out what the items have in common. Then create a category name for each list.

1. Stop Signs

  Blood

  Rubies

  Lipstick

  Roses

  These things are _____

2. Thanksgiving

  Christmas

  Kwanza

  Memorial Day

  Labor Day

  These are all _____

3. Chocolate

  Vanilla

  Strawberry

  Butter Pecan

  Black Raspberry

  These are _____

4. Crazy 8's

  Old Maid

  Go Fish!

  Poker

  Rummy

  These are _____

Match Them Up!

Categories are used in our everyday lives. Where would you expect to find the following items on display? Match the items with the category by writing the letter of the correct category on the line provided.

Items	Categories
1. horror, comedy, drama, action, foreign, games, new releases _____	**a.** restaurant menu
2. fiction, nonfiction, poetry, young adult, children's, reference, newspapers, magazines _____	**b.** video store
3. meat, dairy products, coffee, tea, cereal, bakery, juice, soda _____	**c.** after-school activities
4. department store, food court, game store, toy store, shoe store, arcade _____	**d.** library
5. appetizers, entrees or main dishes, side dishes, salads, desserts, beverages _____	**e.** grocery store
6. basketball, arts and crafts, chess club, school newspaper, cooking fun, math wizards, writing club _____	**f.** mall directory

Classify Animals

Scientists **classify** animals so they are easier to study and to understand. Read the following definitions, and then organize the list of animals into categories. Use reference materials, if needed.

mammals—have live babies and feed their babies with milk

reptiles—have scaly skin, are born on land, and are cold-blooded

arthropods—have more than four jointed legs

amphibians—born in the water with gills, develop lungs, and live on land

birds—have feathers and are born from eggs

spider	man	frog	dog	chicken	ant
whale	ostrich	turtle	robin	lobster	snake
alligator	polar bear	caterpillar	fox	blue jay	toad

Mammals	Reptiles	Arthropods	Amphibians	Birds

That's Classified

People advertise in the classified pages of the newspaper to sell things they no longer want. It is called "classified" because all of the items are put into **classes** or **categories.** That way, people can find what they are looking for without reading through all of the ads. Here are some typical categories.

Furniture	Jobs (Help Wanted)	Pets and Pet Supplies
Automobiles	Musical Instruments	Homes (Real Estate)
Sporting Goods		

Read the sentences below. After each sentence, write the category where that person should look for what he or she wants.

1. Miranda wants a new desk. _____

2. Sam wants a bike but can't afford a new one. _____

3. Mr. Wilson wants a used set of golf clubs. _____

4. Carl wants to buy a drum set. _____

5. Mrs. Jenkins is looking for a dining room set. _____

6. Yukiko wants a new kitten. _____

7. Yukiko also wants a carrier for her kitten. _____

8. Paula wants to look for a summer job. _____

9. The Bensons are looking for a new home. _____

10. Bill wants to buy an inexpensive car. _____

Laundry Day

Fred is doing the laundry. He divides the clothes into two **categories:** whites and darks. He then sorts the two piles into **subcategories** according to whether the laundry can be washed in cold or warm water.

1. What main categories does Fred use to sort the clothes?

   _____

2. Into what subcategories does he sort the clothes?

   _____

3. How many categories of laundry will Fred have? _____

Fred is folding the laundry. As he folds each item, he puts it in a pile for his parents, his brother, his sister, or himself. He also has a pile for kitchen and bathroom towels.

4. Into how many piles (categories) does Fred sort the folded laundry?

   _____

Food Fun

Make a list of twenty of your favorite foods. Be sure to include all food groups.

_____

_____

_____

_____

Next, look at the food pyramid below. This is one way nutritionists **classify** foods. Then put your favorite foods into each category. Which of the categories have the most foods?

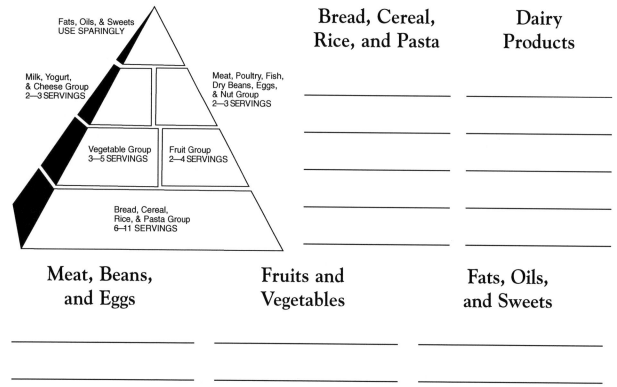

Fats, Oils, & Sweets
USE SPARINGLY

Milk, Yogurt,
& Cheese Group
2—3 SERVINGS

Meat, Poultry, Fish,
Dry Beans, Eggs,
& Nut Group
2—3 SERVINGS

Vegetable Group
3—5 SERVINGS

Fruit Group
2—4 SERVINGS

Bread, Cereal,
Rice, & Pasta Group
6—11 SERVINGS

**Bread, Cereal,
Rice, and Pasta**

_____

_____

_____

_____

_____

**Dairy
Products**

_____

_____

_____

_____

_____

**Meat, Beans,
and Eggs**

_____

_____

_____

_____

**Fruits and
Vegetables**

_____

_____

_____

_____

**Fats, Oils,
and Sweets**

_____

_____

_____

_____

Planting a Garden

Jenny wants to plant a flower garden. She knows that she has to plan her garden so that taller plants are in the back and shorter ones are in front. She decides to put the plants in **categories.** Any plant over 24 inches will be considered tall. Medium plants are from 12 to 23 inches, and short plants are under 12 inches.

Plants	Height	Color
bachelor's buttons	12–18 inches	blue
begonia	6 inches	red
candytuft	4–6 inches	white
daisy	18 inches	white
delphinium	26 inches	blue
iris	12 inches	purple
marigold	6 inches	yellow
sunflower	60 inches	yellow

Help Jenny by listing the plants in three categories: tall, medium, and short.

Tall   **Medium**   **Short**

_____   _____   _____

_____   _____   _____

_____   _____   _____

_____   _____   _____

_____   _____   _____

We Belong

When you **classify,** you group things together in some way. The whole group of items is called a **category.** Classifying can help you organize items. It can also help you organize ideas when you read. Look at the three words in each group below. Write the name of their category on the line. Then add another item to the list.

Words That Belong Together   **Category**

1. whale   dolphin   walrus
   New Item _____   _____

2. soccer   baseball   football
   New Item _____   _____

3. pretty   fantastic   wonderful
   New Item _____   _____

4. sister   brother   mother
   New Item _____   _____

5. Europe   Asia   Australia
   New Item _____   _____

6. a   o   u
   New Item _____   _____

7. car   train   truck
   New Item _____   _____

8. Eric Carle   Leo Lionni   Beverly Cleary
   New Item _____   _____

9. computer   fax machine   desk
   New Item _____   _____

10. apricot   apple   avocado
    New Item _____   _____

The Category Game

Anyone can play the category game. Set a time limit of three to five minutes. Fill in words that fit under each category and begin with the letters shown on the left. You only get points if no one else uses your word. This game can be played with different categories and letters.

	Names	Birds	Food	Forms of Transportation
S				
T				
A				
P				
L				
E				

Wild or Tame

Look at the list of animals and birds below. Then classify them as Wild or Domesticated (tame).

pig	cat	cow	tiger	chicken
dog	rooster	beaver	eagle	sheep
fox	antelope	hamster	guinea pig	zebra
horse	panda	giraffe	blue jay	squirrel

1. Wild

_____ _____   _____ _____

_____ _____   _____ _____

_____ _____   _____ _____

_____ _____   _____ _____

_____ _____   _____ _____

2. Domesticated

Now re-sort the Domesticated Animal list into House Pets or Farm Animals.

3. House Pets

_____

_____

_____

_____

4. Farm Animals

_____

_____

_____

_____

_____

Daily Skill-Builders Reading 4–5
walch.com © 2004 Walch Publishing

They're Different

We **contrast** things by thinking about how they are different from each other. Think of two differences between the items in each pair below and write them on the lines provided.

What's the difference

1. between basketball and baseball? _____
   _____
   _____

2. between summer and winter? _____
   _____
   _____

3. between apples and oranges? _____
   _____
   _____

4. between swimming in a lake and swimming in the ocean? _____
   _____
   _____

5. between riding in a car and riding on a bus? _____
   _____
   _____

6. between talking and listening? _____
   _____
   _____

Two Sisters

Read the following paragraph, and look for ways the sisters are alike and different. Then answer the questions below.

> Two sisters own a candy shop in town. They are both hardworking, and they both love candy. It is a lot of work to own a candy shop. Someone has to make the candy, someone has to sell the candy, and someone has to count the money and pay the bills. The two sisters share all the jobs equally. Amelia, the older sister, is better at making candy. When it is her day to make the candy, the shop is filled with customers, and they sell most of the candy she makes. Ellen is more outgoing than her sister. She always chats with the customers. When it is her day to work at the counter and sell the candy, lots of people stop in to say "hello" and buy some candy. Amelia is much shyer than her sister. Both Amelia and Ellen are good at counting money and paying the bills.

Compare the sisters. Tell three ways they are alike.

1. _____

2. _____

3. _____

Contrast the sisters. Tell two ways they are different.

4. _____

5. _____

Daily Skill-Builders Reading 4–5
walch.com © 2004 Walch Publishing

Space Neighbors

Read the following paragraph, and **compare** and **contrast** Venus, Earth, and Mars. Then answer the questions below.

> Earth has two neighbors in space: the planets Venus and Mars. These planets have some things in common with Earth, but Earth is the only planet in our solar system that supports life. Venus is nearer to the Sun than Earth. Mars is on the other side of Earth, farther away from the Sun. Like Earth, Venus has an atmosphere, but it is too hot to breathe. Venus is covered with clouds that are so thick and dense that heat and carbon dioxide are trapped on the surface. This makes Venus the hottest planet in the solar system, with temperatures over 400 degrees Celsius! Mars has no atmosphere and is covered with a reddish dust. Temperatures on Mars are moderate, like those found on Earth, and can reach above freezing in the summer. Mars is smaller than both Earth and Venus, which are about the same size. Earth has one moon, while Venus has none. Mars has two moons.

1. How are Mars and Venus alike? _____

   _____

2. How are Mars and Venus different? _____

   _____

   _____

3. What is one way Earth is like Mars? _____

   _____

4. Name one thing that Earth and Venus have in common. _____

   _____

5. How is Earth different from both Mars and Venus? _____

   _____

Two Cities by the Bay

Read the following paragraph, and **compare** and **contrast** the cities of San Francisco and Boston.

Visitors to San Francisco, California, often notice how similar the city is to Boston, Massachusetts. Both are quaint, colorful cities filled with historic charm. Both have interesting crooked streets and many beautiful, old buildings. Boston is the capital of its state, while San Francisco is not, but both are located on a waterfront. San Francisco looks out over San Francisco Bay, Boston onto Boston Harbor. Both are important ports—Boston for the Atlantic Ocean and San Francisco for the Pacific Ocean. San Francisco is certainly more hilly and can boast about its famous cable cars. But Boston has many historical points of interest, such as the Old North Church and the Freedom Trail. Both cities are important centers for art and culture.

Complete the Venn diagram to compare and contrast the cities.

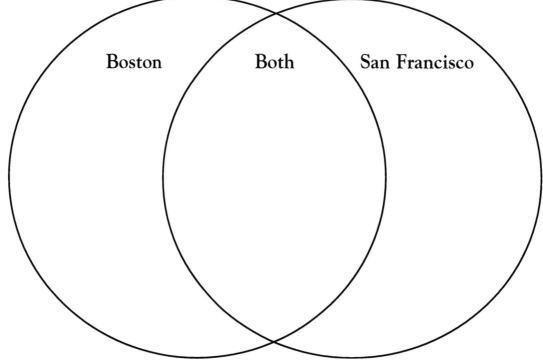

Boston   Both   San Francisco

Tomato Time

Sometimes we want to find out how things are **alike.** That is when we **compare.** If we want to find out how things are **different,** we **contrast.**

Look at the following seed packet information. Compare and contrast the information and answer the questions below.

Shady Lady	**Easy Reds**
Height: 2 feet	Height: 2 feet
Preferences: Part sun or shade	Preferences: Sun
Days to Maturity: 200	Days to Maturity: 60
Size: Tomatoes are 1 inch	Size: Large, round fruits
Color: Yellow/orange	Color: Deep red
Uses: Mostly for decorations	Uses: Great for eating

1. Are these two tomato plants more alike or more different?

   _____

2. Besides both being tomatoes, in what way are they both similar?

   _____

3. Which plant matures first? _____

4. How do the two plants differ in color? _____

   _____

Raccoons and Pandas

Comparing and **contrasting** can help us understand complicated subjects. Scientists compare and contrast in order to increase their understanding of a topic. Read the following paragraphs, and then answer the questions below.

Raccoons are bold and outgoing. Although people have moved into traditional raccoon habitats, raccoons do not seem to be afraid of people. They adapt to city life by eating garbage and living in abandoned buildings or cars. In the wild, they live in hollow trees, old beaver lodges, or haystacks. Raccoons are omnivores, which means that they will eat anything. In the wild, they might feast on fish, insects, fruits, vegetables, and bird eggs. Some animal populations dwindle and become endangered when humans take over their habitat, but the adaptable raccoon has thrived.

Pandas are found only in one small area in the mountains of China. They only eat a certain kind of plant called bamboo. Pandas are an endangered species because people are cutting down the forests where bamboo grows. Pandas are shy creatures and try to stay away from others.

1. How would you contrast raccoons and pandas? _____

   _____

2. What common problem do raccoons and pandas share? _____

   _____

3. What useful quality does the raccoon have that the panda lacks?

   _____

   _____

Daily Skill-Builders Reading 4–5
walch.com © 2004 Walch Publishing

Pet Plans

A fifth-grade class wants to buy a pet for their classroom. They raised $50.00 at a school fair. Their teacher, Mr. Wally, says that they can buy a pet as long as it fits these guidelines: It costs less than $50.00, has a cage or aquarium as its home, weighs less than 20 pounds, and is not too noisy.

Read the chart about possible pets. Then answer the questions that follow.

	Lizard	**Parrot**	**Puppy**	**Rabbit**	**Guinea Pig**
Votes	9	8	8	4	3
Cost	$7	$80	$10	$5	$2
Habitat	aquarium	cage	roams	cage	cage
Characteristics	quiet	noisy	noisy	quiet	mostly quiet
Weight	1 pound	3 pounds	25 pounds	5 pounds	3 pounds

1. Which pet(s) can be eliminated because of cost? _____

2. Which pet(s) can be eliminated because of weight and habitat?

   _____

3. Which pet(s) can be eliminated because of noise?

   _____

4. Of the pet(s) left, which is the most popular? _____

5. Mr. Wally says to eliminate the lizard because of possible bacteria. Which two pets are left to choose from? _____

6. The pet shop owner advises them that guinea pigs can make annoying noises. Which pet should they buy? _____

Making Choices

Matt has to choose a summer camp. Read about the two camps below. Then list at least three differences as you **compare** and **contrast** the camps.

Camp Lots-of-Fun

This is a camp for those who like to have fun. A typical day at Camp Lots-of-Fun begins when everyone gathers in the main lodge to watch cartoons on television. After that we wander down to the lake for swimming fun (we don't have swimming lessons at our camp). Then we order some pizzas for lunch and take naps in our bunks. Each day we have a fun barbecue and a campfire.

Camp Study-a-Lot

Camp Study-a-Lot is for the student who wants to keep up with his or her schoolwork. We have late-night study sessions, group trips to the library, and afternoon study hours. Each camper is required to read three books a week and give an oral report on one of them. Our swimming lessons with lifeguard training are required. For meals, we have cooking lessons, and campers take turns being cooks for the whole camp.

Differences

_____

_____

_____

_____

_____

Daily Skill-Builders Reading 4–5
walch.com © 2004 Walch Publishing

Two Stories

Read and **compare** and **contrast** these two stories. Then answer the questions.

The Ant and the Grasshopper (Aesop's Fable from Ancient Greece)
When the days were long and the sun was hot, the Ant worked busily. She was gathering food and storing it for the winter. At the same time, the Grasshopper was singing and dancing. The Ant warned the Grasshopper that he ought to get ready for winter, but the Grasshopper wouldn't listen. On a cold winter night, the Grasshopper begged the Ant for some food, but the Ant refused. "I worked all summer while you were playing and singing," she said. "I won't give you any."

The Little Mice (from Myths & Legends of the Sioux)
Once upon a time a prairie mouse busied herself all fall, storing away a supply of beans. The little mouse had a cousin who was fond of dancing and talk, but who did not like to work. She was not careful to gather beans, and the season was already well gone before she thought to start gathering. She found she had no packing bag for beans. So she went to her hardworking cousin and said:

"Cousin, I have no beans stored for winter and no bag to gather them in. Will you lend me one?"

"But why have you no packing bag?"

"I was too busy talking and dancing."

"And now you are punished," said the other. "It is always so with lazy, careless people. But I will let you have the bag. And now go, and try to recover your wasted time."

1. How are the two stories alike? _____

_____

2. How are they different? _____

_____

109

City Mouse, Country Mouse

Read the following story. Underline the dangers and discomforts of city and country life as you **compare** and **contrast** the places to live.

Country Mouse was tired of the country living. Every time he went out of his little hole, he feared for his life. There was a hawk and a fox that lived nearby. He was tired of berries but was afraid to venture out. How he longed for the posh city life that his cousin enjoyed. When he got an invitation to visit his city cousin, he was overjoyed. "I'm sure I won't be coming back," he told the Squirrel.

Country Mouse arrived in the city quite late at night and went right to bed. They slept on cushions, in a warm and cozy nook right behind the furnace. He thought back on his cold, damp little hole under the oak tree. In the morning, however, Country Mouse was awakened by a horrible din. "Oh, that's just the Grandfather Clock," yawned his city cousin, going back to sleep. Country Mouse was so upset by the booming gongs that he could not go back to sleep. He decided to creep into the kitchen. Sure enough, cheese was on the counter. He had never tasted anything so delicious. Suddenly, a huge, furry face with whiskers appeared. Country Mouse dropped the cheese and fled back to the furnace. "Oh, that was just the cat," his cousin explained. Country Mouse hardly dared to peek his face out from behind the furnace after that. It was stuffy back there, and he longed for a breath of fresh air. He found himself thinking of the juicy berries that he had enjoyed in the country.

Soon after, Country Mouse sneaked away to his country home, leaving his cousin a nice thank-you note, of course, and bringing a piece of cheese with him for his friend, the Squirrel.

Now compare and contrast the comforts of city life with those of country life. Use the back of this paper.

Daily Skill-Builders Reading 4–5
walch.com © 2004 Walch Publishing

Map Adventures

Maps have keys that explain the symbols and help you figure out what the map is telling you. Look at the map and key below. Then answer the questions.

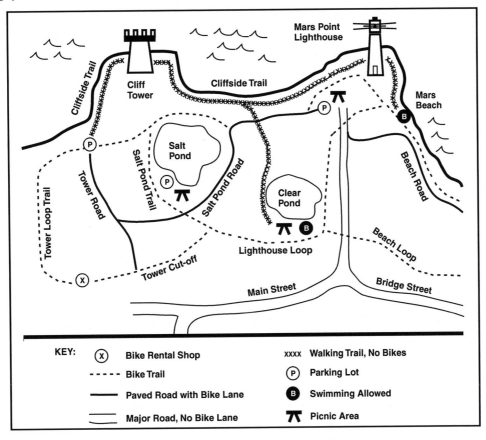

KEY:

Ⓧ Bike Rental Shop	xxxx Walking Trail, No Bikes
- - - - Bike Trail	Ⓟ Parking Lot
—— Paved Road with Bike Lane	Ⓑ Swimming Allowed
Major Road, No Bike Lane	Picnic Area

1. What is the only way to get to the Cliff Tower?

_____

2. Where can you have a picnic?

_____

3. Where can you swim?

_____

4. What is the quickest bike route from the rental shop to Mars Beach?

_____

A New England Map

Maps help us understand the world around us. Look at the following map of New England. Then answer the questions below.

New England

Maine

Atlantic
Ocean

Vermont

New Hampshire

Massachusetts

Connecticut

Rhode Island

1. How many states are in New England? _____

2. Which is the largest New England state? _____

3. Which two New England states border Vermont? _____

_____

4. Which is the smallest New England state? _____

5. Which states must you pass through to go from Maine to Rhode Island?

_____

6. Which New England state does not have a seacoast? _____

Matt's Goals

Matt has set some goals for himself. Look at the **chart** that lists his goals and what he has achieved. Then answer the questions below.

Goals	Monday	Tuesday	Wednesday	Thursday	Friday
Get up with alarm	Y	Y	N	N	N
Feed cat	Y	Y	Y	Y	Y
Do homework	Y	Y	N	Y	—
Practice piano	Y	N	Y	N	Y
Take out garbage	Y	N	Y	Y	Y
Read $\frac{1}{2}$ hour	Y	Y	Y	Y	Y
Total Yes Answers	6	4	4	4	4

1. Did Matt have any perfect days? Which ones? _____

   _____

2. Which goal(s) did Matt accomplish every day? _____

   _____

3. Which goal was the hardest for Matt? _____

   _____

4. How many total yes's could Matt achieve if he accomplished every goal for every day? _____

5. How many yes's did Matt achieve for the week? _____

Mansfield Trees

For Earth Day, the city of Mansfield planted 500 trees. After a harsh winter, the Parks Department created a **chart** to show how the trees were doing.

Tree	Planting Area	Number Planted	Number Alive	Number Dead
birch	downtown	33	20	13
	neighborhoods	50	48	2
	riverside	7	7	0
	roadside	10	0	10
dogwood	downtown	23	15	8
	riverside	38	31	7
maple	neighborhoods	45	40	5
	roadside	40	10	30
pine	downtown	15	15	0
	riverside	27	27	0
	roadside	25	25	0

1. How many birch trees were planted by the roadside? _____

2. How many of the roadside birches are alive? _____

3. How many maple trees were planted? _____

4. How many trees died by the roadside? _____

5. Which tree do you think is the hardiest? _____

6. Which location do you think is the most stressful for trees? _____

_____

Daily Skill-Builders Reading 4–5
walch.com © 2004 Walch Publishing

Graphic Artists

Mrs. Lee teaches art. She likes to keep track of which artist is the most popular among her students over the years. She has created a **bar graph** showing results for the past five years among her students.

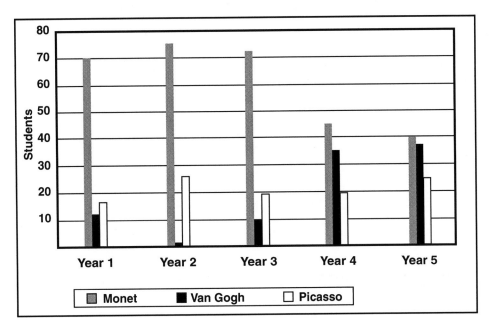

1. Which artist is the most popular in Year 1? Is there one artist who is always most popular? _____

2. Approximately how many students does Mrs. Lee have each year? _____

3. How many painters are included on the graph? _____

4. Mrs. Lee changed her teaching style to emphasize a different artist in Year 4. Do you see a change in Years 4 and 5 that might be caused by her new methods? _____

5. About how many students preferred Van Gogh in Year 5? _____

6. Based on the trend shown in the graph, can you make a prediction about Year 6? _____

Pizza Pie

There are 30 children in Mr. Wong's class. They have done a survey on favorite pizza toppings. The data collected looks like this.

Cheese: 15	Pepperoni: 12	Onions: 3

1. What percentage of the class likes plain cheese pizza? _____

2. What percentage of the class likes pepperoni? _____

3. What percentage of the class likes onion pizza? _____

4. Do the three percent figures add up to 100? _____

5. Look at the **circle graph (pie chart)** below. It is divided into three sections. Which section should represent cheese pizza? Pepperoni? Onion? Use the key to write the correct symbol in the correct section. (**Hint:** You have figured out the percentages in the questions above.)

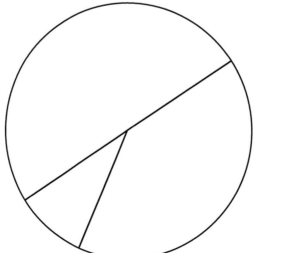

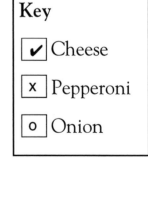

Key

✔ Cheese

x Pepperoni

o Onion

For the Birds

Colin has a part-time job at the pet shop. Customers always want to know the type of wild birdseed to buy for certain birds. To make it easier, he decides to create a **table.** Study the table, and then answer the questions below.

Bird	Cracked Corn	Millet	Safflower	Sunflower	Suet	Sugar Water	Thistle
Blue Jay				X			
Blackbird	X						
Cardinal			X	X			
Chickadee			X	X			
Dove	X						
Finch			X	X			X
Hummingbird						X	
Junco		X					
Nuthatch			X	X			
Sparrow	X	X					
Woodpecker				X	X		

1. Which food is liked by most of the wild birds? _____

2. How many types of birds like thistle? _____

3. Which birds like more than one type of food? _____

_____

4. Which bird likes suet? _____

5. What do hummingbirds like to eat? _____

6. Which bird likes the most different kinds of food? _____

Touchdown!

Jimmy's dad has a season ticket for football games played by the local team, the Lakeville Lancers. He can get an extra ticket for Jimmy for one game. Here is the team's schedule.

Day	Date	Opponent	Time
Sunday	Sept. 7	•Hawks	1 P.M.
Sunday	Sept. 14	•Zebras	4 P.M.
Sunday	Sept. 21	Lions	1 P.M.
Sunday	Sept. 28	•Minnows	7 P.M.
Monday	Oct. 6	Monkeys	9 P.M.
Sunday	Oct. 12	Antelopes	1 P.M.
Sunday	Oct. 19	•Cougars	1 P.M.
Sunday	Oct. 26	Rovers	1 P.M.
Monday	Nov. 3	•Ferrets	9 P.M.
Sunday	Nov. 16	Fiddlers	9 P.M.
Sunday	Nov. 23	•Bluebirds	1 P.M.
Sunday	Nov. 30	•Lobsters	1 P.M.
Sunday	Dec. 7	Otters	4 P.M.
Saturday	Dec. 20	•Lambs	8 P.M.

A bullet (•) indicates an away game. All the rest are home games.

1. How many home games are there? _____

2. How many games are away? _____

3. How many different teams do the Lancers play? _____

4. Which day do the Lancers usually play? _____

5. Jimmy can go to one home game with his dad. His mom says it has to be a Sunday game, at 1:00, so he won't be out too late on a school night. How many games does Jimmy have to choose from? _____

Sail Away

Many sports have their own vocabulary. Look at the **diagram** of a sailboat and answer the questions below.

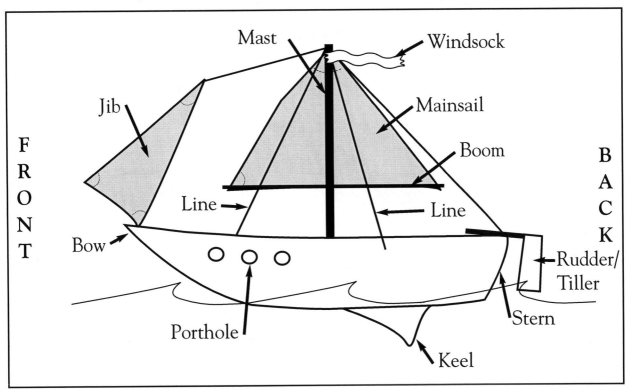

1. What is the front of the boat called? _____

2. What is the back end of the boat called? _____

3. What are the names of the two sails shown? _____

4. What are windows on a boat called? _____

5. What is the part that stretches out the mainsail called? _____

6. What do you call the part of the boat that is beneath the water? _____

_____

The Moving Earth

A **diagram** can make learning easier. Look at the following diagrams. Then answer the questions below.

How Earth's Crust Moves

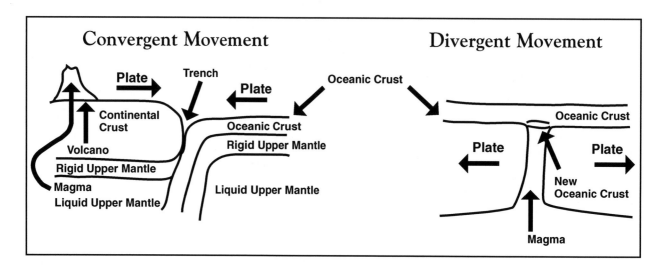

1. Which movement occurs when sections of Earth's crust, called plates, collide or come together? How can you tell?

   _____

   _____

2. When two sections of the Earth's crust are moving apart, what is the movement called?

   _____

3. During which movement are volcanoes formed?

   _____

4. During which movement is new oceanic crust formed?

   _____

What Characters!

Sometimes an author lets a character's actions tell what the character is like. This can make a story more interesting and can help the reader better understand the character. For instance, if the author writes, "Bill was kind," it is not as convincing as if he said, "Bill helped his little sister get back on her bike." Read the following sentences and use clues from the sentences to fill in the lines.

1. "Thank you for bringing me flowers. You are so _____."

2. The firefighter ran into the burning building to save the life of a child. The firefighter is _____.

3. The boy stuffed his mouth and then his pockets with cookies. The boy is _____.

4. You never get your work done! You are _____.

5. She is always smiling. She is _____.

6. Stefan told his brothers to clean up after the other campers; then he told them to stay at the back of the line; then he told them to stop talking. Stefan is _____.

7. Carlos went back into the store to tell the cashier that she forgot to charge him for his comic book. Carlos is _____.

8. The other girls were giggling about the new girl, but Rosie asked her to join them for lunch. Rosie is _____.

9. Even the teacher laughed when Tony told jokes on the bus. Tony is _____.

10. Every time the teacher asked a question, Ray knew the answer. Ray is _____.

Oh, Those Pigs!

Read the following story, and then answer the questions below.

You remember the three little pigs. Their mother sent them off to make their way in the world, and they built houses of straw, wood, and brick. This story takes place months after the wolf was driven away. The pigs are living together in the snug brick house of Practical Pig, who was smart, sensible, and hardworking. This is why he built a house of brick.

One morning Fiddler Pig was watching his mother weed her garden. "Oh, Mother," he complained, "I dislike that cold, damp brick house we live in. How I miss my airy straw house!"

Mother Pig was tired of hearing Fiddler complain. "You are such an ungrateful Pig! Practical took you in and saved you from the wolf!"

The next day, Fifer pig stopped by, looking gloomy as he watched his mother wash windows. "Oh, Mother," he moaned, "How I dislike living in that crowded brick house!"

Mother Pig scolded Fifer. "You are very greedy and selfish to want your brothers out."

Later Practical Pig came to see his mother. He cut firewood. He helped her paint her front door. He did not say a word about his two brothers.

1. What adjective does Mother Pig use to describe Fiddler? Why?

_____

_____

2. What adjectives does Mother Pig use to describe Fifer? Why?

_____

_____

3. What words describe Practical? How do you know he is like this?

_____

_____

Amanda Bean

Read the following paragraph. Look for words that describe Amanda as a negative person. Then answer the questions below.

When Amanda Bean walked into a room, trouble was certain to follow. At Tammy's birthday party on Saturday, Amanda said she was allergic to dogs, so she had to sit on the porch and eat cake. There she was, out on the porch, eating cake all by herself, which put a bit of a damper on the party. Everyone decided that Tammy would open her presents on the porch so Amanda could be included, and every time Tammy opened a present, Amanda would claim to already have that gift, or say that her mother didn't think that it was a safe toy. Of course, everyone else was looking at the toy and wondering what she meant by unsafe. Tammy looked as though she might cry, and her mother was looking at the clock a lot.

1. Does the author want you to like Amanda? How do you know?

   _____

2. Circle one word from the list below that describes Amanda.

selfish	greedy
kind	mean
inconsiderate	unhappy
generous	insecure

3. What is an example from the paragraph that explains why you chose that word?

   _____

   _____

   _____

   _____

Four Sisters

You can tell a lot about characters from what they do and say. Little Women, by Louisa May Alcott, is a story about four sisters. The story begins with the four girls talking. See what you can guess about the girls from what they say and do.

> "Christmas won't be Christmas without any presents," grumbled Jo, lying on the rug.
>
> "It's so dreadful to be poor!" sighed Meg, looking down at her old dress.
>
> "I don't think it's fair for some girls to have plenty of pretty things, and other girls nothing at all," added little Amy, with an injured sniff.
>
> "We've got Father and Mother, and each other," said Beth contentedly from her corner.

Answer the questions about the four sisters. Find words in the paragraph that give you clues to their character, and write them to help explain your answers.

1. Which sister is content with what she has? _____

_____

2. What does Meg wish for? _____

_____

3. Why is Jo "grumbling"? _____

_____

4. Do the sisters seem unhappy? Why or why not? _____

_____

5. Which sister do you like best? Why? _____

_____

Where Are We?

Setting is the place where a story happens. Read the following descriptions, and write what kind of place is being described.

Paragraph I	**Paragraph II**
The air was cool and fresh, with a spicy scent. Different bird calls and whistles were the only sounds, except for the faint sound of water trickling. The tall pine trees were almost black against the bright blue sky, and it was cool beneath their branches. The ground under their feet was soft and spongy with pine needles.	Horns were blaring. A bus roared by, blocking the sun and letting out a blast of fumes. The pavement was hard. There were so many smells coming from the delicious foods of street vendors and flowers sold on street corners. Crowds of people filled the sidewalks and surged across the streets once the lights changed.

1. We are in _____.   2. We are in _____.

3. Now, list some things that were described in each paragraph.

Paragraph I   Paragraph II

_____   _____

_____   _____

_____   _____

_____   _____

4. Which setting appeals to you more and why? Use examples from the paragraphs to explain. _____

_____

_____

Set the Scene!

How important is the **setting**? Some stories could take place anywhere. Other stories rely more on the setting. Sometimes, as in the following paragraph, the setting is the story.

> Dark spruce forest frowned on either side of the frozen waterway. The trees had been stripped by a recent wind of their white covering of frost, and they seemed to lean towards each other, black and ominous, in the fading light. A vast silence reigned over the land. The land itself was a desolation, lifeless, without movement, so lone and cold that the spirit of it was not even that of sadness. It was the Wild, the savage, frozen-hearted Northland Wild.

This paragraph is from <u>White Fang</u> by Jack London. It is about a dog that is part-wolf and grows up in the wilds of the North. The cold, harsh land is a place where animals and people have to fight for survival. Notice how the forest "frowns," how the trees seem "to lean towards each other"; the Wild seems almost to be a living character in the story. Obviously, this story could not be moved to a different climate without losing much of its meaning.

1. What are some words in the paragraph that help you to visualize the setting? _____

   _____

2. Why do you think Wild is capitalized? _____

   _____

3. Could this story take place in a different climate or setting? Why or why not? _____

   _____

Perfect Setting?

Think about a book you have read recently. How important was the setting in this book? Remember that **setting** has to do with time and place.

Book: _____

Author: _____

1. Write a detailed description of the setting. _____
   _____
   _____
   _____
   _____

2. Was the setting important to the story? Why or why not? _____
   _____
   _____
   _____

3. Can you imagine the story in another location? Why or why not?
   _____
   _____
   _____

4. Can you imagine the story in another time period? Why or why not?
   _____
   _____
   _____

Kansas or Oz?

In <u>The Wonderful Wizard of Oz</u> by Frank L. Baum, the **setting** is very important to the story. Read the paragraphs below. One describes Kansas, and the other describes Oz.

When Dorothy stood in the doorway and looked around, she could see nothing but the great gray prairie on every side. Not a tree nor a house broke the broad sweep of flat country that reached to the edge of the sky in all directions. The sun had baked the plowed land into a gray mass, with little cracks running through it. Even the grass was not green, for the sun had burned the tops of the long blades until they were the same gray color to be seen everywhere.

The cyclone had set the house down very gently—for a cyclone—in the midst of a country of marvelous beauty. There were lovely patches of greensward all about, with stately trees bearing rich and luscious fruits. Banks of gorgeous flowers were on every hand, and birds with rare and brilliant plumage sang and fluttered in the trees and bushes. A little way off was a small brook, rushing and sparkling along between green banks, and murmuring in a voice very grateful to a little girl who had lived so long on the dry, gray prairies.

1. Which setting appeals to you? Where would you rather live and why?

   _____

   _____

2. Dorothy has one wish—to get back home to Kansas. When she is finally back on the dull, gray prairie she says, "There's no place like home." Why do you think she preferred Kansas to Oz?

   _____

   _____

Plot Mountain

The **plot** of a story is simply what happens, or the action. It is a series of events that occur in a certain order to form a story. You can think about a plot as if you were climbing a mountain. The action "rises" as events move toward a turning point or **climax.** Let's look at the plot of the familiar fairy tale "Cinderella."

> **a.** The Prince invites all the ladies in the land to a ball.
> **b.** The Stepmother won't let Cinderella go to the ball.
> **c.** A Fairy Godmother appears and helps Cinderella go to the ball.
> **d.** The Prince dances with Cinderella and falls in love with her.
> **e.** She runs off at the stroke of midnight, leaving one glass slipper.
> **f.** The Prince uses the glass slipper to find Cinderella.
> **g.** They get married and live happily ever after.

1. What is the turning point of the story, that is, the climax of the action?

_____

2. Look at the mountain shape below. Notice the very top of the mountain. This is the climax of the plot. Use the letters from the list of events above to label the plot mountain.

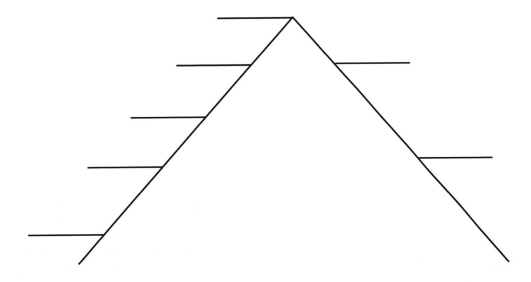

Problems, Problems

Plots are driven by conflict. A **conflict** is a problem. Without some problem that has to be solved (resolved), there would be no story.

Problem/Conflict
The jealous queen hates her beautiful stepdaughter.

Resolution
The stepdaughter is rescued by the prince.

Read the following story beginning. Think about what the problem is and how it might be resolved.

> Larry was walking to school one day when he saw something shiny on the sidewalk. It was a watch, a nice one! It was shiny and had a stopwatch button, and other fancy dials. He picked it up and slipped it over his wrist. It fit perfectly. Larry had been wanting a watch. He checked the time as he approached the school. It felt good to glance at a watch on his wrist and know the time. Now, he knew he was not late for school. A few people noticed his watch during the day, and Larry showed it off with pride. Then, as he was leaving school, he heard some girls talking. "Oh, he's going to beat up the person who took it!" "It belonged to his grandfather; it's really valuable." Larry suddenly knew they were talking about the watch. At the bottom of the steps was Kendall Coville, the worst bully in the school. He looked angry. He looked ready for a fight. Larry recognized some of the boys at his side. One of them had asked about Larry's watch just about an hour before. Larry had showed him how the stopwatch worked.

1. What is the problem? _____

   _____

2. What does Larry do that causes the problem? _____

   _____

3. How do you think the problem can be resolved? _____

   _____

What If?

Thinking about the **plot** helps you understand what message the author wants to tell. We all know the story "Cinderella." Think about the plot of the story and try to imagine how the story might have been different.

Examples: What if Cinderella's wicked stepmother was not wicked at all? (_Cinderella would have had a happy childhood._)
What if Cinderella didn't lose her glass slipper on the palace steps? (_The prince might not have found her._)

Read the following summary of "Jack and the Beanstalk," and write some "what if" sentences of your own.

> Jack and his mother were very poor. One day Jack's mother told him to take their cow to the market and sell it so they could buy some food. She warned Jack to be sure to get a good price for the cow. Jack ended up trading the cow for three magic beans. His mother was furious when he came home with just the three beans. Jack planted the beans anyway, and in the morning there was an enormous beanstalk. He climbed up to a giant's castle and managed to steal a goose that could lay golden eggs. The giant chased Jack down the beanstalk, but Jack managed to get to the bottom and cut it down first. The giant was killed in his fall from the beanstalk, and Jack and his mother lived happily ever after.

1. What if _____

2. What if _____

3. What if _____

4. If there were no bad stepmothers or if Jack was not foolish, what would happen to these stories? Would they be as interesting? _____

_____

Motivation

Plots are often driven by character motivation. **Conflicts** are often caused because one character wants something and someone or something else gets in the way.

In <u>The Wizard of Oz</u>, Dorothy's motivation for her journey was her wish to return to her home and family.

List four movies or books that you have recently seen or read. For each one, list a main character and something that he or she wanted that caused the plot to move forward.

1. _____

_____

_____

2. _____

_____

_____

3. _____

_____

_____

4. _____

_____

_____

Sleepyhead!

When the **point of view** in a story is in the **first person,** the author uses _I._
When a story is in the **third person,** the author uses _he, she, it,_ and _they._
Write **1** for **first person** or **3** for **third person** at the end of each of the
following sentences.

1. For a long time, I used to wake up early. Now I sleep late every day. _____

2. Mark woke up early and called his friends. They all agreed to meet at the beach. _____

3. Mark's mother was thinking that they should be home by 3:00 P.M. She worried about them when they went to the beach. _____

4. I was having a bad dream. _____

5. The beach was beautiful and peaceful that day. _____

6. Kevin finally got out of bed at 11:00 o'clock in the morning. _____

7. When I got out of bed, it was 11:00 o'clock; I was still tired. _____

8. Mark's mother made them sandwiches to take to the beach. _____

9. I dreamed that the school warning bell was ringing and ringing. _____

10. Over at Kevin's house, the phone was ringing. _____

11. "He's probably still asleep," thought Mark, as the phone rang. _____

12. I was rushing to get to class, but I kept going the wrong way. _____

13. Mark and his friends went to the beach without him. _____

14. I couldn't believe they went to the beach without me! _____

15. I tried to call Mark, but his mother said they had already left. _____

16. Mark's mother felt bad for Kevin. "Why don't his parents make him go to bed earlier?" she wondered. _____

Who Is Speaking?

Even when the **point of view** of a story is in the **third person,** characters in conversation can talk about themselves in the **first person.** As you read the story, fill in the lines. Then answer the questions below.

John and Fred were arguing over the last candy bar.

"It's mine!" cried _____, "I saw it first!"

"It's mine!" screamed John, "You had one already!"

"Give it to me," demanded _____, as John managed to get the candy bar away from him.

"No!" said _____, hiding it behind his back.

Ben was trying to watch television, but looked up when the twins raced into the room. They chased each other and wrestled on the floor.

"What's going on?" asked _____.

They both spoke at once. All Ben could hear was something about a candy bar.

"Why don't you split it?" _____ suggested.

John and Fred looked at each other.

"Okay," said Fred.

"Okay," agreed _____. But when John drew the candy bar out of his pocket, the chocolate was melted and mashed.

"Too bad," said _____. "Now neither of you gets any candy."

1. Who is telling the story? _____

2. Is the story told in the first or third person? _____

3. How many people are in the story? _____

4. Who are the twins? _____

5. Who do you think Ben is? _____

Beach Vacation

Read the paragraphs below, paying attention to **point of view.** Then answer the questions that follow.

Ben, Bonnie, and Bart had been friends their whole lives. They were all the same age, except Bonnie was a month older than Ben and Ben was a month older than Bart. One year, when they were all twelve, their families went on vacation together. They went to the beach for a week. Ben liked to lie in the hammock before lunch and read a book, but Bart and Bonnie liked to collect shells along the beach. Bonnie liked to go for long walks before breakfast, but Ben and Bart liked to play catch in front of the house. At night, they all liked to sit by the campfire and toast marshmallows. They all agreed it was the best vacation ever!

1. Who is telling the story above? Is the person telling the story one of the characters in the story? _____

2. Whose thoughts do we learn about? _____

I am lucky, because I have two best friends. Their names are Ben and Bart. We are all the same age, except I am one month older than Ben and two months older than Bart. We have been friends for our whole lives. For my twelfth birthday, my parents took us all to the beach for a whole week. We had a great time. I took a walk by myself every morning before breakfast. Later in the morning, Bart and I collected shells. We got a book from the library and looked up the different shells we found. At night, we would toast marshmallows by the campfire. We all thought it was the best vacation ever!

3. Who is telling this story? _____

4. In this story, do we know what Ben or Bart are doing or thinking when Bonnie is not with them? _____

John and the Elf

Authors have to decide what **point of view** to use when writing a story. Sometimes the main character uses *I* (**first person**) to tell the story.

John's Story

I was walking to school one day, when suddenly a mean-looking elf leaped out of a tree and blocked my way. I was scared and threw my backpack at him. Of course, he disappeared before the bag hit him and then started throwing rotten apples at me from a tree branch. While I was running, I lost my backpack. No one believed my story. I am never walking that way to school again.

Whose is the point of view in the above story? _____

Now write the story from the elf's point of view, using *I* for the elf. Remember, when you write in the first person, you can only get one person's point of view.

The Elf's Story

_____

_____

_____

_____

_____

_____

_____

_____

Daily Skill-Builders Reading 4–5
walch.com © 2004 Walch Publishing

Name that Theme

The **theme** of a story is the idea that connects all of the other ideas in the story. Read these paragraphs, and answer the questions that follow.

> Carol is having a party. She has decorated her house with red and green streamers and pictures of apples. She is serving apple pie, apple bread, apple cookies, and apple cider. She is wearing a white dress with pictures of apples on it. All of her guests will receive a small basket of apples as a party favor.

1. What is the theme of Carol's party? _____

> When you walk into Juan's room you might think you were walking into a space station. There are posters of planets and stars; model spaceships cover every shelf. The curtains and bedspreads have moons and stars on them. The ceiling is painted black with glow-in-the-dark stars. There is a telescope set up by the window, and one whole wall is painted to look like the surface of the moon.

2. What is the theme of Juan's room? _____

> On Monday, the teacher announced, "Today begins National Poetry Month. We are going to study poetry in many different ways and in every subject. For instance, we will apply math skills to analyze poems. We will illustrate poems in art class. We will research famous poets in social studies, and we will find and read poems about science for science class."

3. What is the theme that will connect everything the children study this month? _____

Theme Match

Some **themes** show up over and over again. Look at the classic themes below and match each theme with a story summary.

---

a. Good against evil

b. Inner qualities are more important than looks.

c. Some go from rags to riches.

d. There's no place like home.

e. Love conquers all.

f. Money can't buy happiness.

_____ **1.** A hideous monster forces a poor man to send his beautiful daughter to live with him. She is afraid at first, but gradually learns that he is kind and noble under his ugly features.

_____ **2.** An evil emperor is trying to take over the earth. He uses aliens who can disguise themselves as humans and take over people's minds. A group of friends finds out about the plot and have to battle the aliens for the sake of humankind.

_____ **3.** A young girl is tired of living on a farm in the middle of nowhere. Everything seems dull and gray and boring to her. One day a tornado sweeps her up and deposits her in a beautiful land. She has many adventures as she tries desperately to get back home again.

_____ **4.** A poor boy grows up to value only money. He works his whole life to save money, never marries, never shares his wealth, only to find when he is old that he is lonely and friendless.

_____ **5.** A young girl is treated badly by her stepmother and stepsisters. She is made to do all the work of the house and is not invited to the Prince's ball. A fairy godmother helps her get to the ball, and the Prince falls in love with her.

_____ **6.** A beautiful young girl has a spell cast upon her by an evil witch. She lies as still as death until the Prince who loves her comes along. He restores her to life with a kiss.

Slow but Steady

A fable is a short story that teaches a lesson. The lesson or moral of the story is also its **theme.** The characters in a fable are usually animals who speak and act like humans. Read the fable below and answer the questions that follow.

The Hare and the Tortoise

One day, a hare made fun of the short feet and slow pace of the Tortoise, who replied, laughing: "Though you be swift as the wind, I will beat you in a race." The Hare, believing this to be simply impossible, assented to the proposal, and they agreed that the Fox should choose the course and fix the goal. On the day appointed for the race, the two started together. The Tortoise never for a moment stopped, but went on with a slow but steady pace straight to the end of the course. The Hare, lying down by the wayside, fell fast asleep. At last, waking up and moving as fast as he could, he saw the Tortoise had reached the goal and was comfortably dozing after her efforts. Slow but steady wins the race.

---

1. What is the theme of the fable? _____

_____

2. Think of another fable and its lesson, or theme. _____

_____

_____

Team Theme

The **theme** is the main idea of the story. Read the following story and try to determine the theme. Underline words or phrases from the text that support your claim. Then complete the sentence below.

Go, Team!

Kenny was eager to get out on the soccer field. He tied and retied his black cleats and did some deep breathing. He was the high-scorer on the team, and his hope was to achieve 30 goals before the end of the season. The coach was giving his usual pregame lecture on teamwork, but Kenny wasn't listening. He was imagining himself kicking the ball into the net for the winning goal.

"So, remember," the Coach was saying, "working together as a team is what it's all about. That's how you win games, that's how you enjoy the game more, and that's how you all become better players. Kenny, you'll be goalie today," he added, handing Kenny the special goalie equipment.

Kenny was stunned. How could he make goals if he was guarding their own net? How could his team even win, if he wasn't out there scoring the goals?

"But, Coach," he protested, "We need to win this game."

The Coach gave him a look. "You know the rules. Part of being on the team means you have to take a turn at being goalie."

"But…but…the team needs me…they need me to score the goals." Kenny knew he should be quiet, but couldn't help himself.

"Are you thinking of the team, or of yourself, Kenny?" asked the Coach.

The theme of this story is _____

_____

_____

Daily Skill-Builders Reading 4–5
walch.com © 2004 Walch Publishing

Showing Emotion

Good readers notice the **tone** of what they are reading and can describe it using just the right adjective. Look at the following list of adjectives describing emotions. Make sure you understand what each word means before proceeding.

angry	sweet	bitter	sympathetic
excited	tired	peaceful	cold
serious	worried	flattering	joyful
eager	urgent	complaining	wistful
sad	frightened	happy	joking
sarcastic	upset		

Decide what emotion best describes each of the following sentences. Choose one or two words for each. Some words might be used more than once.

1. "What a beautiful day!" _____

2. "I wish I could just go home and stay in bed all day." _____

3. "Why doesn't anyone ever listen to me?" _____

4. "Stop it, right now!" _____

5. "How I miss my sister when she goes to camp." _____

6. "Oh, you think you're so smart." _____

7. "I think it's about time you finished your work." _____

8. "Oh, let's hurry up and get to the fair!" _____

9. "Help, help!" _____

10. "Oh, no, I can't believe I left my wallet at home!" _____

Tone of Voice

Has a parent or teacher ever said, "Don't use that **tone** of voice."? A certain tone of voice means you are showing some emotion by the way you speak. Sometimes one's tone gives a different meaning to the spoken words.

> **Example:** "I'm so happy," said Jade in a *dull* voice.
> The word *dull* changes the meaning of what Jade said.

Sometimes a writer uses descriptive words to tell how something is said. Read the following dialogue. Underline the words that describe tone of voice. Then answer the questions below.

"Hurry up, Tim," called Amy in an impatient voice. "We're waiting!"

"I'm coming," replied Tim. He sounded anxious. "I can't find my wallet."

"Oh, great!" Amy cried angrily. "Here we go again. Every time we are going somewhere, we have to wait for you to find something."

"I'm sorry," muttered Tim sarcastically. "I wish I was perfect like you." He finally located his wallet under the mail on the kitchen table, and they went out the door. Kelly was waiting in the driveway. "Ready to go?" she asked eagerly, climbing on her bike and beginning to coast along the sidewalk. "Oh, it's a beautiful day for a bike ride," she sang happily.

Amy was still annoyed. "Tim is so slow," she complained. "I'm tired of waiting for him."

"He's not doing it on purpose," Kelly said soothingly. "Don't be angry."

---

1. When Amy says, "Oh, great!," how do you know she doesn't really mean that something great has happened? _____

   _____

2. When Tim says "I'm sorry," does he really sound sorry? How do you know? _____

   _____

3. How is the tone different when Kelly speaks? _____

   _____

Daily Skill-Builders Reading 4–5
walch.com © 2004 Walch Publishing

Author's Tone

The way the author writes a story often results in a certain tone. The **tone** gives readers clues about an author's attitude. Read the following paragraph. Be aware of the author's tone. Then answer the questions that follow.

Once long ago in a time when life was easier than it is now, there lived a king and queen who lived in the most joyous kingdom on earth. The king was a kind and loving person. He would look forward each day to touching the hearts of all those he encountered—including his beautiful wife. At times, however, the queen became jealous of the attentions the king would give to others. When the loving king sensed his wife's jealousy, he would take her by the hand and say, "Oh, beautiful wife, the most beautiful woman in all the land. I love you above everyone and anything else." The queen would pretend to be assured, but down deep she feared the king's devotion to his kingdom.

1. How would you describe the author or narrator's tone? Is he or she serious or amused? Is the tone light or heavy?

   _____

   _____

2. What do you think the author's attitude is toward the king? Toward the queen?

   _____

   _____

   _____

Nonfiction Tone

Nonfiction writing is based on facts, but you should not believe everything you read! Nonfiction writing can inform, persuade, instruct, or advise. In some cases, the author may use facts or leave out facts to persuade the reader. The author's **tone** can be an important clue about the author's attitude toward the subject. Read both paragraphs. Then answer the questions that follow.

A. **Selection from <u>Gardener's Handbook</u>**
Rudbeckia: common name is black-eyed Susan. An easy-to-grow perennial flower with sturdy stems and many blossoms. Rudbeckia is a favorite in the flower garden and combines well with other summer-bloomers, such as Phlox or Daylilies. Will spread to fill in an empty space in your border and provide color all summer long, even during dry spells.

B. **Article from a garden column in the weekly newspaper**
Fellow gardeners, I urge you to rethink your flower garden this year. I, for one, am tired of the roadside weed called rudbeckia, otherwise known as "black-eyed Susan." Do you really want to look at cheerful, yellow flowers all summer? They need no care and require no skill. A self-respecting gardener should not even consider this plant.

1. Which paragraph includes mostly facts? _____

2. Which paragraph includes opinions? _____

3. In which paragraph does the author try to persuade? _____

4. In which paragraph does the author try mostly to inform? _____

5. In which paragraph does the author convey a negative tone? _____

6. In which paragraph does the author convey a neutral tone? _____

What Is a Genre?

Books are often classified as fiction or nonfiction. Within those two categories, writing is also classified by type, or **genre.**

Common Genres

Fiction—writing that tells stories that are not based on facts

    Historical Fiction—set in another time period, using some actual people or events as part of the story

    Science Fiction—set in the universe, usually in the future

    Detective or Mystery—has clues, crime, detectives

    Fantasy—set in made-up worlds, with made-up characters

    Fairy Tales—fantasy tales that have been handed down for generations

    Horror—frightening things that happen to ordinary people

Nonfiction—writing about events or topics that are based on facts

    Biography—a type of nonfiction written about a person

    Autobiography or Memoirs—written by a person about that person's life

---

Help the characters find their genres. Write the correct genre on the line next to each statement.

1. I am a detective; I look for clues. _____

2. My name is Abraham Lincoln. This is my life's story. _____

3. I am a princess. I am looking for a prince. _____

4. I am a space warrior. I keep evil aliens away. _____

5. I will tell you the story of Abraham Lincoln. _____

6. My name is Sadie. I was a spy in the Civil War. _____

7. I live in the secret Kingdom of Nar. _____

8. I spent the night in a haunted house and was chased by monsters.

_____

Why Do We Read?

People read for many reasons: to learn more about a subject, to find out how to do something, to learn about a famous person's life, and for the pure enjoyment of it. People read many different **genres,** or types of writing. Written works are classified into **fiction,** writing that is made-up or imaginary, and **nonfiction,** writing that is true or based on fact. But there are sub-genres of these two categories, too.

Look at the following sub-genres, and then write **F** for Fiction or **NF** for Nonfiction next to each one. Answer **Y** for yes if you have read this type before and **N** for no if you have not. Then write why you think someone might read a book in that genre.

Genre	Fiction or Nonfiction	Read (Y/N)	Why read this genre?
1. Poetry			
2. Biography			
3. Historical Fiction			
4. Dictionary			
5. Mystery			
6. Myth or Legend			
7. Science Fiction			
8. Horror			
9. Encyclopedia			
10. Fairy Tale			
11. Cookbook			
12. Fantasy			
13. Newspaper Article			

Daily Skill-Builders Reading 4–5
walch.com © 2004 Walch Publishing

Librarian for a Day

Suppose you were asked to fill in for the school librarian. The librarian says that people will come in today to pick up their books. Each book below is of a certain **genre.** Match each book with the correct request.

a. Easy Classroom Recipes	**f.** Encyclopedia of Animals
b. Space Alien Adventures	**g.** Manual of Small Building Projects
c. The Missing Agent	
d. Fun Fables for All Ages	**h.** Voyage to a Distant Planet
e. U.S. Presidents: Lives and Times	**i.** The Life of Sally Vole, Astronaut

1. Billy from Mrs. Pearson's second-grade class needs to write a report about a United States president. _____

2. Connie likes stories with clues, crimes, and detectives. _____

3. Mrs. Valejo wants to read a short story that teaches a lesson to her class. _____

4. Third-graders need information about animals for a class project. _____

5. Mr. Fitz, the science teacher, wants a book on how to build a birdhouse. _____

6. Miss Torres wants to make cupcakes with her preschool class. _____

7. The fourth grade is starting a science fiction book club and needs two books from which to choose. _____ or _____

8. Karen from the fifth grade is going to do an extra-credit book report about a modern woman's life. _____

Thinking About Genre

Genre affects how we understand what we read. For example, if we pick up a science fiction book, we would automatically prepare ourselves for spaceships, interplanetary travel, strange creatures, fantasy, and excitement. So, we are able to understand something about character, plot, and setting simply by knowing the genre.

Genres	
myth/legend	newspaper editorial
autobiography	fable
fairy tale	mystery
encyclopedia article	cookbook

Match the genres in the box with the characteristics listed.

1. castles/enchanted woods
   princes/princesses
   fairies/witches
   magic spells
   Genre: _____

2. persuasive tone
   reconstructing scene of the crime
   facts used to support opinions
   on a special page of the newspaper
   Genre: _____

3. teaching a lesson
   animals acting human
   Genre: _____

4. first person narration
   facts about someone's life
   Genre: _____

5. gods/goddesses
   explanation for things in nature
   supernatural or magic events
   Genre: _____

6. recipes
   colorful pictures
   ingredients
   Genre: _____

7. detectives/suspects
   reconstructing scene of the crime
   crimes/clues
   priceless objects stolen
   Genre: _____

8. facts about a subject given
   tone is detached and formal
   opinions are not expressed
   overview of subject
   Genre: _____

A Day at the Fair

Sensory language appeals to our five senses. Authors use sensory language to help readers imagine the setting and get more involved in the story. Read the following paragraph, and underline all the sensory words that you find.

It's fun to go to the fair. Oh, the sights and smells! Hot dogs and sausages are sizzling and filling the air with a spicy aroma; popcorn is popping with a buttery scent; sticky cotton candy is melting, all sugary-sweet, in your mouth and clinging to your fingers and face. Balloons are dancing on their strings or breaking with loud "pops" or else sailing away into a cloudless sky. People are screaming as the roller coaster sweeps them downward from the top of the sky. The carousel goes up and down and round and round. Carnival workers are shouting, "Three tries for a dollar," and you feel the hot sun on your back and people's shoulders jostling yours as you watch three clowns juggling and tumbling.

Now, write two words from the paragraph for each sense.

1. Taste   _____   _____

2. Touch   _____   _____

3. Sound   _____   _____

4. Sight   _____   _____

5. Smell   _____   _____

Painting with Words

Just as a painter carefully chooses the right color when painting a scene, a writer chooses just the right word when writing. Words are to a writer as colors are to a painter. Just like color, some words have shades of meaning.

Examples: Tai is _sad._   Tai is _miserable._

Sad and _miserable_ have similar meaning, but _miserable_ has a specific _shade_ of meaning.

Read each of the paragraphs. Then answer the questions that follow.

> **A.** Karla was nervous. She was tired of waiting for her turn and just wanted to get it over with. Finally, her name was called. She went up to the stage, took out her poem, and began to read. When it was over, she sat down with a smile of relief.

> **B.** Karla was terrified. Her palms were sweaty, and her heart was pounding. When she walked up on the stage, it seemed to sway under her feet. When she got to the podium, she took out her poem. When she opened her mouth to speak, no words would come out.

1. Which paragraph gives a better sense of how Karla feels? _____

2. What sensory words does the author use in the second paragraph to tell the reader how Karla feels?

   _____

   _____

3. The author uses the words _nervous_ and _terrified_ to describe how Karla feels. How are these words the same? How are they different?

   _____

   _____

   _____

Daily Skill-Builders Reading 4–5
walch.com © 2004 Walch Publishing

Choosing the Mood

The author sets the **mood** of the story through careful **word choice.** Consider the following examples. For each one, write the mood or feeling that is created and think about the word choices that create the mood.

> It was a hot, overcast day. The gray sky had a yellowish tinge and seemed to press down on the earth. There was scarcely a breath of air, and the leaves on the trees hung lifelessly down.

1. The mood is _____

2. How would the meaning change if there was a hot wind blowing?

   _____

> Clara crouched in the darkness, heart pounding. Her breath came in gasps from her run through the cemetery. She strained her eyes to see something, anything in the blackness that surrounded her. She knew she had been followed.

3. The mood is _____

4. What if Clara is trying not to giggle? _____

   _____

> It was a calm night. There was no moon, and the sky seemed immense, black, and pinpointed with billions of stars. The boat rocked gently on the waves, and there was no sound except the gentle slap of water against the side.

5. The mood is _____

6. What if the night were eerily calm instead of just calm? _____

   _____

Decisions, Decisions

Authors choose their words carefully. **Word choice** can make the author's tone friendly and casual or formal and serious.

> **Examples: Formal language**—more serious and solemn, uses more complex words; usually written in third person.
>
> **Informal language**—casual and fun, shorter, easier words; uses first (I) or second person (you).

Imagine your older sibling is looking into colleges. Compare two college brochures. Note word choice and tone. Then answer the questions.

A. Edgewood College is where a talented and hardworking young person can shine. The small campus makes it possible for a student to become involved in college life and to make friends with many students. Edgewood is a peaceful place for a student to enjoy a quality education. Prospective students are invited to visit Edgewood, the right place for the motivated, high-achieving student.

B. We think you're going to like Bartleby College. We're big! At Bartleby, you'll be one of thousands, and you'll feel the lively lifestyle of a big city. As one of the larger schools in the state, we offer a long list of programs. You want football? We've got it. Marching band? We've got the best. You want to have fun while still getting a pretty good education? We were voted the most fun school in the East for the last five years! Come on out and visit us!

---

1. Underline any words that you do not understand. Are there more difficult words in paragraph A or B? _____

2. Which person is each paragraph written in? Which one uses second person? _____

3. Which paragraph is more formal? What word choices create a formal tone?

_____

As Fast As a . . .

Authors use similes to make their writing more lively and interesting. The sentence "Big Red was as fast as the wind" gives the reader a more colorful image than "Big Red was a fast horse." **Similes** use *like* or *as* to compare two things that are not really alike (a horse and the wind). Complete each simile by filling in a word from that fits the list below.

diamonds	coal	apples	lion	candy	ice
monkey	wind	desert	silk	drum	hornet

1. Your hands are as cold as _____!

2. That runner is as fast as the _____.

3. The air is soft like _____.

4. Her rosy cheeks were like _____.

5. The little boy ran around like an active _____.

6. Her eyes shone like _____.

7. My heart was pounding like a _____.

8. He roared like a _____.

9. My throat is as dry as the _____.

10. The cat is as black as _____.

11. She is as sweet as _____.

12. The teacher is as mad as a _____.

Check It Out

A **metaphor** is used to compare things without using like or as. *That girl is an angel!* You could also use a simile to say *that girl is like an angel* or *as good as an angel*. Make a check (✔) next to each sentence below to tell whether it contains a simile or a metaphor.

	Simile	Metaphor
1. The little boy was a whirlwind.		
2. The house was as neat as a pin.		
3. He's as steady as a rock.		
4. He's a rock!		
5. The ocean is a big bathtub.		
6. Your room is a pigsty!		
7. She is like a computer.		
8. He's a walking computer!		
9. You're as good as gold!		
10. It is as hot as an oven outside today.		
11. The air outside was like an oven.		
12. The house was an oven.		

Daily Skill-Builders Reading 4–5
walch.com © 2004 Walch Publishing

Hairy, Scary

Read the following story to learn what **hyperbole** means. Then answer the questions below.

"It's huge! It's enormous! It's scary! It's hairy!" cried the children together or one at a time, some standing on their chairs, some scurrying to the other side of the room. "It's a monster!"

"Now what's all the hyperbole about?" asked Mr. T., putting down his briefcase.

"It's a spider!" cried the class all at once, pointing at a really rather large, rather hairy, rather scary spider that was dangling from the ceiling above Mr. T.'s desk. Mr. T. quickly stepped back and told the children to assemble near the door. "Keep an eye on it," he commanded and hastily dialed the number of the science teacher's room. "Mrs. Ortiz?" he spoke into the receiver. "Please come at once. There is something here that might interest you." He turned his back to the class to whisper into the receiver, "Yes, it's huge. It's a monster. It's hairy. It's scary. Please help."

Presently, Mrs. Ortiz arrived panting. "Oh," she cried, when they pointed out the spider to her. "It's magnificent! It's…it's…monumental!" She shed a tear at the sight of the enormous, hairy, scary, monstrous, magnificent, monumental spider dangling delicately above Mr. T.'s coffee cup. It didn't take Mrs. Ortiz long to capture the spider, and with the class trailing behind her, they brought the spider outside and placed it in a pleasant spider habitat.

1. What do you think hyperbole means? _____

2. Who uses hyperbole in the story? Underline examples of hyperbole.

_____

3. Do you ever exaggerate when telling a story? Why do you think people exaggerate? _____

_____

Person, Place, or Thing?

Personification gives human qualities to something that is not human. For example, _The car refused to start._ Personification is often found in poetry. Read the poems below and answer the questions.

> Beside the laughing brook I stood
> And gazed upon the frowning wood.
> The stream whispered "stay, stay,"
> But the woods commanded me their way.

1. What two natural things are being personified in the little poem above? What do the things do that make them seem human? _____

_____

_____

> Justice blindly rules
> And sheds a goodly light
> On nations where liberty
> Is each person's right.

2. What idea is being personified in the second poem? What human qualities are used? _____

_____

_____

> The birds were singing good-morning
> As the crickets bade us good night
> And the lantern closed his single eye
> As we sat in the early light.

3. What three things are personified above? _____

_____

4. Look at the poems, and name two categories of things that can be personified. _____

Idioms

All languages have **idioms.** These are figures of speech whose meanings have become widely accepted through use. We use idioms so frequently that we might not notice how odd they sound to someone who is learning English.

Example: It's a **piece of cake.** (It's easy.)

Match the following idioms (in italics) with their literal meanings.

1. You're _playing with fire._ ___

2. I _caught some Z's_ during class. ___

3. He's as _sharp as a tack._ ___

4. I feel _like a fish out of water._ ___

5. Are you _pulling my leg?_ ___

6. Whew, that was a _close call!_ ___

7. Stop _beating around the bush._ ___

8. What happened? _I'm all ears!_ ___

9. Don't _count your chickens before they hatch._ ___

10. Okay, let's _call it a day._ ___

11. _Sooner or later_ you will have to study. ___

12. She just _rubs me the wrong way._ ___

13. Don't _make a mountain out of a molehill!_ ___

14. That's pretty _far-fetched._ ___

a. annoys me

b. count on uncertain things

c. eventually

d. taking unnecessary chances

e. exaggerate the problem

f. took a nap

g. a narrow escape

h. extremely smart and quick

i. unbelievable

j. stop working

k. eager to listen

l. out of place

m. avoiding the subject

n. joking

Spice Cabinet

Jenny is going to label and **alphabetize** the spice cabinet. She bought a set of labels and cut them up. Now she has to stick them on the bottles and put them in alphabetical order. Help Jenny put the spices in alphabetical order.

Cumin	Mace	Basil	Paprika
Oregano	Thyme	Nutmeg	Tarragon
Marjoram	Cardamom	Allspice	Cinnamon

ABC's of the South

Look at the map of these southern United States. Put the states in **alphabetical order.** Below each state, list its largest cities in alphabetical order.

1. State _____

   Cities: _____, _____, _____

2. State _____

   Cities: _____, _____, _____

3. State _____

   Cities: _____, _____, _____

4. State _____

   Cities: _____, _____, _____

5. State _____

   Cities: _____, _____, _____

6. State _____

   Cities: _____, _____, _____

Presidential ABC's

Look at the following list of twentieth-century United States presidents.

McKinley	Roosevelt (F. D.)	Carter
Roosevelt (T.)	Truman	Reagan
Taft	Eisenhower	Bush (G.)
Wilson	Kennedy	Clinton
Harding	Johnson	Bush (G. W.)
Coolidge	Nixon	
Hoover	**Ford**	

List the last names of the presidents in **alphabetical order.** One president is done for you.

A-J

1. _____

2. _____

3. _____

4. _____

5. _____

6. _____

7. Ford

8. _____

9. _____

10. _____

K-Z

11. _____

12. _____

13. _____

14. _____

15. _____

16. _____

17. _____

18. _____

19. _____

Daily Skill-Builders Reading 4–5
walch.com © 2004 Walch Publishing

Winter and Summer

The Winter and Summer Olympics Committees have mixed up their sports! Separate the sports into a Winter and a Summer list. Then **alphabetize** each list.

swimming, cross-country skiing, bobsled racing, gymnastics, rowing, baseball, ice hockey, horseback riding, archery, luge, canoeing, high diving, sailing, figure skating, tennis, alpine skiing, volleyball, speed skating, ski jumping, track and field, cycling, snowboarding

Winter	Summer

Using the Dictionary

Dictionaries tell us everything we need to know about a word: how to pronounce, spell, and use a word, and what part of speech the word is.

Example: tempo *n.* the speed of a piece of music

Abbreviations

adj. — adjective   interj. — interjection   pron. — pronoun
adv. — adverb   n. — noun   v. — verb
conj. — conjunction   pl. — plural

Read these dictionary entries. Then answer the questions below.

> **burn** 1. *v.* to set on fire 2. *n.* an injury caused by heat, fire, the sun, or the wind
>
> **but** 1. *conj.* however; on the other hand 2. *prep.* except, apart from (everyone won but me) 3. *adv.* only
>
> **butter** *n.* yellow substance made from cream or whole milk
>
> **buttery** *adj.* like butter
>
> **bye** *interj.* good-bye

1. *But* has several different meanings and uses. List the parts of speech that *but* can be used for.

   _____

2. Which word is an adjective?

   _____

3. Which word can be both a verb and a noun?

   _____

4. How many syllables are in the sample word *tempo?*

   _____

Dictionary Practice

Some words have more than one meaning. Read these **dictionary** entries.

---

grass *n.* 1. green plant with long, narrow leaves, eaten by grazing
  animals 2. plant with seed like fruit, such as wheat or rye

grate *v.* 1. grind into small pieces by scraping 2. to rub against another
  object with a harsh sound 3. to irritate, annoy

grate *n.* frame of metal bars

gray *adj.* a color made from mixing black and white

Answer the following.

1. Look at the entry for *grass*. Circle the numbers *1* and *2* in the entry. How
   are the two definitions different? How are they the same?

   _____

   _____

2. Look at the first entry for *grate*. Circle the numbers *1*, *2*, and *3* in the
   entry. Are the definitions more alike or different?

   _____

   _____

3. Can you explain why *grate* is listed twice, but *grass* is only listed once?

   _____

4. Write a sentence using *grate* in one of the ways given in the first entry.

   _____

5. Write another sentence using *grate* as it is defined in the second entry.

   _____

Pronounce It

A **dictionary** tells you how to pronounce a word as well as what the word means and how to spell it. Every dictionary has a key, or guide to pronunciation symbols. Look at the following pronunciation key.

Pronunciation Key

ă fat, lap
ā ape, late

ä car, father

ĕ ten
ē meet

ĭ is, hit
ī file

ŏ lot, mop
ō go, cone
ô born
o͞o tool
o͝o book
oi oil, boy
ou out

ŭ up, cut
ū use
ur fur, burn

ə a in ago
  e in agent
  i in sanity
  o in comply
  u in focus

Now look at the following definitions.

above (ə buv) *adv.* higher, overhead
cove (kōv) *n.* small, sheltered inlet or bay
glove (gluv) *n.* covering for the hand
grove (grōv) *n.* a small group of trees
love (luv) *n.* deep affection for someone or strong interest in something
move (mo͞ov) *v.* change place or position
rove (rōv) *v.* to roam or wander

1. Check the pronunciation key. Do any of the words rhyme? Which ones?

   _____

   _____

2. Which word does not rhyme with any of the others?

   _____

Daily Skill-Builders Reading 4–5
walch.com © 2004 Walch Publishing

Look It Up!

Dictionaries have **guide words** at the top of each page that show you where to find a word. Guide words show the first word on the left page and last word on the right page. Look at the list below. Then write the correct words from the list on each dictionary page between the guide words where you would find them. If a word cannot be found on the pages given, circle it.

engage	capital	lily	library	nightingale
nettle	entity	delude	palace	pun
bowling	latent	carriage	protein	formal
famous	larkspur	nickel	navy	delirious
prove	district	extra	punctual	carrot
blare	engine	bingo	blemish	carp
foreign	delta	bleed	elevator	formidable

1. Blanket — Bless

2. Carpet — Cartoon

3. Delicate — Deluge

4. Enemy — Envelope

5. Forever — Fortune

6. Lariat — Latin

7. Nectar — Nocturnal

8. Pronoun — Punctilious

A Little Quiz

What do you already know about using a **table of contents?** Complete the following by circling the letter of the correct answer.

1. Which of the following might have a table of contents?
   a. a novel
   b. a science textbook
   c. a magazine
   d. all of the above

2. What do you use a table of contents for?
   a. enjoyable reading
   b. word definitions
   c. to figure out what a book contains
   d. all of the above

3. What can you learn from a table of contents?
   a. approximately how many pages are in a book
   b. how to find the index in a textbook
   c. what the book might be about
   d. all of the above

4. To *preview* a book means
   a. looking at the table of contents to see how many chapters it contains.
   b. reading over the chapter titles and making predictions about the plot.
   c. looking at the front and back covers and reading the notes on the back.
   d. all of the above.

5. A magazine's table of contents tells you
   a. how many articles are in the issue of the magazine.
   b. who wrote each article.
   c. the page number to turn to for each article.
   d. all of the above.

6. Where would you turn to find what page a chapter begins on?
   a. the index
   b. the glossary
   c. the table of contents
   d. all of the above

Preview and Predict

Look at this **table of contents** and answer the questions that follow.

Chapter One	The Old Sea Dog	11
Chapter Two	Black Dog Appears	18
Chapter Three	The Black Spot	35
Chapter Four	The Sea Chest	51
Chapter Five	The Last of the Blind Man	68
Chapter Six	The Captain's Papers	70
Chapter Seven	I Go to Bristol	83
Chapter Eight	The Voyage	99
Chapter Nine	Council of War	115
Chapter Ten	My Island Adventure	123
Chapter Eleven	The Ship Is Abandoned	139
Chapter Twelve	The Attack	166
Chapter Thirteen	My Sea Adventure	193
Chapter Fourteen	Gold!	221
Chapter Fifteen	The Enemy Camp	254
Chapter Sixteen	The Treasure Hunt	267
Chapter Seventeen	Homeward Bound	278

(adapted from Treasure Island by Robert Louis Stevenson)

1. Do you think this table of contents is from a fiction or nonfiction book?

   _____

2. How many chapters are in this book? _____

3. About how many pages are in this book? _____

4. What point of view is the book written in, and how do you know?

   _____

5. What do you think the book is about?

   _____

6. Would you like to read this book? Why or why not?

   _____

   _____

Lost Contents

Some **table of contents** items have been lost. Decide where the items in each table of contents should go. Then draw a line to the correct picture.

1. Division Facts
   Addition and Subtraction
   Measurement
   Graphing
   Geometry

2. Comics
   Crosswords
   Editorial
   Television/Radio
   Weather

3. The Early Settlers
   The Thirteen Colonies
   The Native Americans
   The Revolutionary War
   The New Nation

4. A Strange Thing Happens
   Who Did It?
   A Clue Is Found
   A Mysterious Stranger
   The Case Is Solved

5. Appetizers
   Soups and Stews
   Salads
   Main Courses
   Side Dishes
   Desserts
   Index of Recipes

Daily Skill-Builders Reading 4–5
walch.com © 2004 Walch Publishing

Using a Table of Contents

Look at this **table of contents** and answer the questions that follow.

1. What kind of book is this table of contents from? _____

2. Which unit do you think is the longest? Why?_____

   _____

3. About how many pages are in the book? _____

4. On what page would you find the chapter on plants? _____

5. On which page would you find a word meaning? _____

Using an Index

An **index** is a way to organize information so that it can be found easily. Look at the following page taken from an index and answer the questions below.

A
Addition
    associative property of, 10
    commutative property of, 8
    of decimals, 396, 402
    of fractions, 277–283
    mental math, 41
    of mixed numbers, 223–227
    of money, 44–47
    practice, 12
    of time, 111–112
    trading, 39–42
Angles, 219–221
Area, 132–133
Associative Property,
    of addition, 10
    of multiplication, 159

D
Dollars and cents. *See* Money.
E
Equations
    addition, 4
    subtraction, 7
Estimating, 210–212, 288
    area, 130
    fractions, 227
    products, 188, 190–191
    quotients, 192-193
Even and odd numbers, 15, 101
F
Fact families
    addition and subtraction, 8–9
    multiplication and division,
    121–122

1. What kind of book is this index from? _____

2. How are the index topics organized? _____

3. Under what topic would you find dollars and cents? _____

4. On what page would you find information on these topics?

    a. estimating area _____
    b. mental math _____

    c. even, odd numbers _____
    d. fact families _____

    e. angles _____
    f. addition of time _____

Busy, Busy Librarian

Read the following story. Then answer the questions below.

Mrs. Klingman, the assistant librarian, was having a busy day trying to process new books. But she kept getting interrupted.

First, Dara Smith came in. "I need to find a map of the Thirteen Colonies," she said. "I can't find it in my social studies book."

Mrs. Klingman opened Dara's book, found the page that read *Index to Maps*, and read off the page number. "Page 55, Dara," she said briskly. She found the page that read *Index to Topics* and said, "That's where you'll find more information on the colonies."

A few minutes later, Colin and Corey appeared at her desk. "How can we find what chapter is about magnets?" they asked. "We have a test coming up." Mrs. Klingman opened their science book from the back, scanned the words listed under "M" in the index and said, "Pages 67–72 or page 79."

"Oh, Mrs. Klingman," Miss Eldridge, the fourth-grade teacher called out, "Can you help me?" She was having trouble finding information on the CD-ROM encyclopedia she had installed. "Check the On-line Index," Mrs. Klingman suggested. She glanced at the clock, "Oh, good, it's lunchtime. The library is closed!" But poor Mrs. Klingman did not go to lunch. She stayed at her desk to finish her work.

1. How many types of indexes are in the story above? _____

2. Can a book have more than one index? Why? _____

_____

3. What should Mrs. Klingman do to make her job easier? _____

_____

4. What index would you use if you wanted information about
   a. the Civil War? _____
   b. a poem by Lewis Carroll? _____
   c. a map of Cuba? _____
   d. Utah state history? _____

Knowledge Collections

Encyclopedias are a series of books (or CD-ROMs) that contain information about everything! The next time you are at the library, take a look at an encyclopedia.

A group of students is researching animals for a school project. See the volumes below from which they can choose to do their research.

Volume I	Volume II	Volume III	Volume IV
Aardvark–Chalk	Champion–Czech Republic	Dagger–Erosion	Estimation–Gymnasium

Volume V	Volume VI	Volume VII	Volume VIII
Gypsy–Motor	Motto–Quicksand	Rapids–Tiger	Tigris River–Zoo–Index

Here are the students and the animals they have chosen. Write the correct volume number that each student should use on the line provided.

1. Anna—aardvark   Volume _____

2. Ricardo—flying squirrel   Volume _____

3. Sonya—anteater   Volume _____

4. Sophie—alligator   Volume _____

5. Kerry—dingo   Volume _____

6. Ken—leopard   Volume _____

7. Violet—chimpanzee   Volume _____

8. Melody—zebra   Volume _____

CD-ROM Power!

Encyclopedias are also available on CD-ROMs. These discs contain as much information as a dozen heavy volumes, and the information is easy to find. Your library probably has a CD-ROM encyclopedia that you can use. If you look on a CD-ROM encyclopedia, you will be able to click on a letter to find an index of topics that begin with that letter. It looks like this:

A/B/C/D/E/F/G/H/I/J/K/L/M/N/O/P/Q/R/S/T/U/V/W/X/Y/Z

If you click on the letter /L/, you will probably see a list of letters similar to this:

LAC/LAG/LAK/LAT/LAV/LEB/LEM/LEW/LIN/LOC/LON/LUD/LYD

You would use alphabetical order to find your topic.

Examples: Lace   click LAC
Ladybug   click LAC
Lagoon   click LAG
Laos   click LAK

Which letters would you click on to find information on these topics?

1. Abraham Lincoln _____

2. Lewis and Clark _____

3. Latvia _____

4. lie detector _____

5. leopards _____

6. Louisiana _____

7. Little Sioux River _____

8. lynx _____

Good Work, Joe!

An **encyclopedia** is an excellent resource when researching a topic. Encyclopedias can give an overview of a subject and help identify, narrow, or broaden a topic. Read the following story, and answer the questions below.

Mrs. Riley has asked the class to write a paper about the Civil War. The Civil War is too broad a topic. There would be too much to cover in ten pages. So each student must use encyclopedias and narrow that topic.

Joe goes to the library to research his topic. He uses an encyclopedia CD-ROM. He searches "Civil War." The encyclopedia comes up with 677 entries, including civil wars in other countries. Joe has to limit his topic and searches "American Civil War."

Still finding 101 entries, Joe then searches for "Abraham Lincoln and the Civil War." He gets seven entries. He chooses his topic, "President Abraham Lincoln, The War Years."

1. Why do you think that Mrs. Riley was so pleased with Joe's topic?

   _____

2. Why do you think that Mrs. Riley did not approve the topic "Soldier's Uniforms"?

   _____

3. Why do you think that Mrs. Riley did not approve the topic "Art, Science, and Medicine During the Civil War Years"?

   _____

4. How do you think the encyclopedia helped Joe limit his topic?

   _____

Types of Encyclopedias

Some **encyclopedias** cover many topics and many categories. There are encyclopedias, however, that focus on one subject and cover that subject in depth. Match the encyclopedias with the topics on the right by writing the letter of the correct topic on the line provided.

Encyclopedias

___ 1. Garden Plants

___ 2. Marine Mammals

___ 3. Coins

___ 4. Dog Breeds

___ 5. Books and Reading

___ 6. Shipwrecks

___ 7. Language

___ 8. Food

___ 9. Volcanoes

___ 10. Civil War

___ 11. Roman Emperors

___ 12. Space Exploration

Topics

a. exploring the moon

b. date of the Emancipation Proclamation

c. the Latin name of a lily

d. Who invented popcorn?

e. a golden retriever

f. Mount Vesuvius eruptions

g. Who wrote <u>Tom Sawyer</u>?

h. migration patterns of whales

i. when the alphabet was invented

j. what Nero did while Rome burned

k. the value of a rare Buffalo nickel

l. early Spanish shipwrecks

What Are Almanacs?

Almanacs began as calendars that showed past weather patterns and astronomical data. Many almanacs predicted the weather and gave seasonal advice to farmers. The first almanac was published in the 1500s. Ben Franklin wrote <u>Poor Richard's Almanac</u> in 1732. The world-famous <u>Old Farmer's Almanac</u> started in 1792. Modern almanacs are published yearly with information on many subjects.

World almanacs give updated information about countries. **Political almanacs** keep track of political changes. **Sports almanacs** tell about sports figures and statistics.

What kind of almanac would you use to find the following information? Write the letters of the correct almanacs on the lines provided.

World Almanac (WA)	Political Almanac (PA)	Weather Almanac (W)	Sports Almanac (SA)

1. Tonya wants to know the scores of the 1974 World Series. _____

2. Jeffrey wonders if it snowed the day he was born. _____

3. Sydney wants to read a speech of a U.S. president. _____

4. Tina wants to know the population of Mexico. _____

5. Mr. Thomas wants to know when he can plant corn. _____

6. Seth can't remember the name of the seventh continent. _____

7. Luis wants to find out who was governor in Texas in 1973. _____

8. Beth wants to know the rules of soccer. _____

Mystery Tides

Miss Carina Todd is writing her seventeenth mystery novel. She is thrilled with the plot. Her detective, the clever Willard Fox, comes to a quaint harbor town for a vacation, but has no sooner arrived when the town's world famous tower clock is stolen. Of course, Fox must find the thief and solve the crime. Miss Todd is trying to tell about the crime. It is necessary to the plot that the crime be committed on a summer night, after 8:00 P.M., at high tide. After that, an important clue must be discovered at low tide at sunrise. Since her loyal readers love her accurate settings, she decides to consult an **almanac** to see if this is possible.

Day	Date	High Time	High Time	July Tides Low Time	Low Time	Sunrise	Sunset
Tue	8	5:03 A.M.	5:39 P.M.	11:59 P.M.	11:06 A.M.	5:05 A.M.	8:24 P.M.
Wed	9	6:12 A.M.	6:43 P.M.	12:05 A.M.	12:01 P.M.	5:05 A.M.	8:23 P.M.
Thu	10	7:16 A.M.	7:41 P.M.	1:01 A.M.	1:12 P.M.	5:05 A.M.	8:22 P.M.
Fri	11	8:21 A.M.	8:40 P.M.	2:08 A.M.	2:15 P.M.	5:06 A.M.	8:22 P.M.
Sat	12	9:25 A.M.	9:38 P.M.	3:10 A.M.	3:17 P.M.	5:07 A.M.	8:22 P.M.
Sun	13	10:25 A.M.	10:35 P.M.	4:09 A.M.	4:15 P.M.	5:07 A.M.	8:21 P.M.
Mon	14	11:21 A.M.	11:30 P.M.	5:05 A.M.	5:10 P.M.	5:08 A.M.	8:21 P.M.

1. How many high and low tides are there each day?

   _____

2. Based on the tide table above, what night(s) could Carina Todd have the crime happen?

   _____

3. What morning(s) can the clue be found?

   _____

Thesaurus Time

A **thesaurus** is a reference tool. It is a dictionary of synonyms—words that have the same or similar meanings. A thesaurus helps writers use new, fresh words instead of tired, over-used words like nice, interesting, or boring!

Look at the entries in the thesaurus below. Then rewrite each sentence, replacing the underlined word with a new one.

> **good,** excellent, admirable, superb, splendid, wonderful
> **good,** obedient, well-behaved
> **nice,** pleasant, agreeable, friendly
> **nice,** warm, sunny, pleasant, lovely
> **interesting,** appealing, glamorous, enthralling, engrossing,
>   entertaining, absorbing, fascinating
> **boring,** tedious, uninteresting, monotonous, unexciting, tiresome

1. The teacher said the book was <u>good</u>.

   _____

2. He is a <u>good</u> boy.

   _____

3. She is so <u>nice</u>.

   _____

4. It is a <u>nice</u> day.

   _____

5. That movie was <u>interesting</u>.

   _____

6. Oh, school is so <u>boring</u>.

   _____

Atlases for All

An **atlas** is a book of maps.

A **street atlas** shows cities and towns with an index to road or street names.

A **world atlas** is filled with maps showing the different countries. World atlases will usually include physical maps and political maps.

> *Physical maps*: maps that show geographic features, such as mountains, valleys, vegetation, and water
> *Political maps*: maps that show political boundaries

An **historical atlas** gives maps that illustrate historical events.

A **sky atlas** shows maps of the stars, showing their positions at different times of the night and during different seasons.

1. What hobby might require you to buy a sky atlas?

   _____

2. To find the country Mount Everest is in, which atlas would you use?

   _____

3. What kind of map would you use to find a mountain range?

   _____

4. What kind of atlas would show how to get to the next town?

   _____

5. What kind of map—physical or political—would need to be updated after a year or so?

   _____

6. What atlas would show where the planet Mars is located?

   _____

Which One to Use?

If you were the reference librarian, which books would you recommend to people looking for the following things? (**Hint:** Some books will be used more than once.) Write the letter of the correct reference book on each line provided.

_____ 1. a poem by Walt Whitman

_____ 2. the date of the full moon next month

_____ 3. the definition of _pessimism_

_____ 4. the location of a street in the next town

_____ 5. a synonym for _happy_

_____ 6. a map showing populations of states in 1876

_____ 7. general information on bats

_____ 8. the high tide on Saturday

_____ 9. maps with current country populations

_____ 10. an overview of the Civil War

_____ 11. information about Abraham Lincoln

_____ 12. constellations that can be viewed in July

a. dictionary

b. poetry anthology

c. sky atlas

d. encyclopedia

e. almanac

f. world atlas

g. thesaurus

h. historical atlas

i. street atlas

Daily Skill-Builders Reading 4–5
walch.com © 2004 Walch Publishing

Answer Key

READING COMPREHENSION

Page 1: Guessing Game
Animal descriptions should include size/shape, color/description, habitat, and food.

Page 2: Build an Aquarium!
Instruction words underlined: Draw, Put, Add, Draw, Fill, Add, Feed. Drawing instructions should be followed.

Page 3: Brush Those Teeth!
Possible answers:
1. Pick up your toothbrush. 2. Put toothpaste on your toothbrush. 3. Brush your bottom teeth. Brush all parts of the teeth. 4. Rinse your mouth out with water. 5. Brush your top teeth. Brush all parts of the teeth. 6. Rinse your mouth out with water. 7. Brush your tongue. 8. Rinse your mouth out. 9. Rinse your toothbrush. 10. Put your toothbrush back where it belongs. 11. Put the toothpaste back where it belongs.

Page 4: Sandwich Chef
Instruction words—Ingredients: cut, cut, sliced *Directions:* preheat, separate, toast, spread, sprinkle, place, put, broil Recipes will vary but should include title, sensible ingredients, and directions with instruction words.

Page 5: Five or More a Day
Posters should include five different fruits or vegetables in five different colors: (red, green, yellow, orange, and blue or purple). Examples: apple, lettuce, banana, orange, grapes, peppers, lettuce, corn, pumpkin, beets

Page 6: Diamante Poems
Poems will vary but should contain opposites and correct parts of speech.
Possible answer:

Winter
Cold, dreary
Shivering, slipping, sliding
Icicles, snowflakes, flowers, butterflies
Swimming, sunning, skipping
Warm, pleasant
Summer

Page 7: Haiku
Senses affected by first haiku—sight, smell, hearing. Second haiku should be divided into syllables as follows: Small/mouse/, gray/ and/ white, /Creep/ing,/ quiv/er/ing,/ stop/ping./ A/ cat/ is/ prowl/ling. Students' poems should have the correct number of syllables on each line. Encourage students to use adjectives and action verbs to create an image.

Page 8: Solar Quest
By using the Sun's location and following directions, students should be able to label the planets in order from the Sun: Mercury (G), Venus (W), Earth (BL), Mars (R), Jupiter (O), Saturn (Y), Uranus (A), Neptune (T), Pluto (BR).

Page 9: Map It Out!
Maps and directions will vary.

Page 10: Tanisha Gets Tricked
1. Many students finished before Tanisha because they followed instructions. 2. Tanisha should have read the whole paper before answering the questions.

Page 11: At the Mall
Underline sequencing words: First, Then, Next, Then, After that, Next, Finally. 1. Candy Corner, 2. Blair's Card Shop, 3. music store, 4. Darla's Designs, 5. bookstore, 6. pet shop, 7. Vinny's Video Games.

Page 12: Chicken Little's Soup
1. In the spring, they have to dig up the dirt and plant the vegetables. 2. In the summer, they have to water the vegetables and pull up the weeds. 3. In the fall, they have to pick the vegetables. To make soup, they have to cut up the vegetables and stir the pot.

Page 13: Maple Syrup Days
1. b 2. c 3. d 4. e 5. a

Page 14: Pet Frenzy
9:00 A.M.: Munchkin, fresh water and one can of cat food; fish, sprinkle of food; 12 P.M.: Munchkin, cat treat; 2:00 P.M.: Mitchell—1 cup birdseed with Tabasco sauce; 5:00 P.M., three dogs get 1 can of dog food each.

Page 15: Follow the Leader!
The parade should be arranged in this order: police car, Brass Band, Recycling float, Scouting float, Drum Majorettes, fire trucks, and Garden Club float.

Page 16: Life-Cycle Sequence
Steps to be underlined: Lay eggs, eggs hatch into caterpillars, caterpillar forms a pupa, butterfly emerges from pupa.
1. egg 2. caterpillar 3. pupa 4. butterfly

Page 17: An Impossible Journey
1. e 2. g 3. d 4. b 5. a 6. f 7. c

Page 18: A Shakespearean Sequence
1. First, Romeo goes to the ball. 2. At the ball, he meets Juliet, and they fall in love. 3. Romeo and Juliet decide to get married secretly. 4. Juliet takes a secret potion that

makes it seem as if she is dead. 5. Romeo kills himself.
6. Juliet kills herself.

Page 19: Your Own Time Line
Time lines will vary.

Page 20: Fire Drill
1. g 2. c 3. b 4. f 5. l 6. m 7. j 8. i 9. a 10. k 11. h
12. d 13. e

Page 21: Topic Talk
1. Topic: rivers; Main Idea: *A river is a very important body of water on Earth.* 2. Topic: mammals; Main Idea: *Many mammals live and thrive in the Pacific Ocean.* 3. Topic: precipitation; Main Idea: *Precipitation can be any kind of water that falls from the atmosphere.*

Page 22: Create Topic Sentences
The topic sentence should include the given topic and a viewpoint or general statement about the topic. Suggested sentences: 1. It is important to have good dental habits.
2. George Washington was one of our greatest presidents.
3. Watching television can be educational. 4. Hobbies help people of all ages relax. 5. Teachers should give less (or more) homework.

Page 23: Ask Aesop
Moral: *Do not attempt too much at once.*
1. The boy's problem is that he can't get his hand out of the cookie jar. 2. He has to decide whether to let go of some cookies or remain with his hand in the jar.
3. Examples of a rewritten moral: *Don't be too greedy* or *Don't try to do too much at once.*

Page 24: A Persuasive Idea
1. Topic: bats; Main Idea: *Bats deserve more respect.* Topic sentence could be rewritten: *Bats should be treated better by humans,* or *Humans should think better of bats.* 2. The writer is trying to tell us that it is dangerous to talk on a cell phone while driving. 3. Topic: cell phones; Main Idea: *Talking on a cell phone is distracting to a driver.* Topic sentence could be rewritten: *Cell phones are dangerous to use while driving,* or *Driving and using cell phones don't mix.*

Page 25: Reading to Learn
1. The topic is glaciers. 2. The main idea is how glaciers move. 3. The author is informing, not persuading.
4. Rewritten main idea: *The movement of glaciers is slow, but fascinating,* or *Scientists learn a lot from the study of the way glaciers move.*

Page 26: Questioning to Learn
1. Charles Lindbergh 2. flew his plane, The Spirit of St. Louis 3. across the Atlantic Ocean from New York to Paris 4. 1927 5. to prove that he could, to advance aviation 6. He flew 30 plus hours without sleeping.

7. Modern aviation owes its beginning to Charles Lindbergh, or Charles Lindbergh became a hero in 1927 when he made the first solo flight across the Atlantic.

Page 27: Finding the Main Idea
1. forest rangers 2. watch out for fires, help tourists, keep park clean, lead tours 3. in National Parks 4. not relevant
5. if you like people and nature 6. get a college degree in appropriate field 7. Students should answer all questions except "when." 8. Sample topic sentence: Someone who likes nature and people would make a good forest ranger.

Page 28: What's Your Hobby?
1. It is about outdoor hobbies. 2. Bird-watching and stargazing are the two other hobbies mentioned. 3. The three hobbies are all done outdoors and are relaxing.
4. They all help people relieve stress, unwind, and relax.
5. The details about each hobby tell about the benefits of being outside and having a hobby. 6. A good title might be "Relax in the Great Outdoors," "Get Outside and Relax," or "Outside Hobbies Can Relieve Stress."

Page 29: Say What You Mean
The main idea is (b). Supporting details pointing to topic sentence: Companies know people will pay more for a scarce toy. Gold is hard to find and is the most valuable metal. Natural pearls are harder to find and more valuable than cultured.

Page 30: The Big Idea
Paragraph 1, main idea: *There is a link between music skills and math skills.* Paragraph 2, main idea: *People who learn to play a musical instrument learn a lot more than how to play notes.* Paragraph 3, main idea: *Even if a person does not show a lot of musical talent, learning to play an instrument is still valuable.* Big Idea: Everyone should learn to play a musical instrument. Sample titles: "Make Music!" or "Music Education for All!"

Page 31: Pizza or Ice Cream?
1. We should have pizza instead of ice cream at the party.
2. Pizza is the most popular food; it is less messy than ice cream; it is easier to serve; it is healthier. 3. Ice cream would be better than pizza at the end-of-school party.
4. Sample supporting details: Ice cream is more fun; no one will be hungry for pizza if the party is after lunch; pizza is more expensive; pizza gets cold too fast; ice cream is better on a hot day.

Page 32: Allergy Season
1. a 2. a 3. b 4. a 5. a 6. b

Page 33: For the Birds
1. Y 2. Y 3. Y 4. N 5. Y 6. N 7. N 8. Y 9. N 10. N

Page 34: Main Idea Ferry

Main idea: *A ferry is a special kind of boat.*
Sample details: They carry cars as well as people; they can be used instead of driving over a bridge; they travel on oceans, rivers, and lakes; they often have snack bars; cars can drive onto one side and drive off of the other side.

Page 35: Popping Popcorn

1. *Popcorn has a long and interesting history.* 2. Popcorn has been around for over 5,000 years; Native Americans used popcorn for food and to make flour; popcorn became a popular snack food in 1800s; the invention of corn-poppers increased ease and popularity; popcorn was the first food to be cooked in a microwave oven; popcorn is the number one selling snack food in the world.

Page 36: Notice the Details

1. c 2. b 3. b

Page 37: Painting Details

Detail sentences: 3, 4, 5, 6, 7

Page 38: A Whale of a Tale

1. The paragraph is about whale migration. 2. Humpback whales travel nearly as far, from Alaska to Hawaii, a round-trip journey of about 6,000 miles. 3. Possible answer: Humpback whales travel nearly 6,000 miles on a round-trip migration from Alaska to Hawaii.

Page 39: Bear Necessities

1. b 2. a 3. a 4. b 5. c 6. b 7. b or N 8. b 9. a 10. c 11. a 12. N 13 a 14. N 15. b

Page 40: Marvelous Mushrooms

1. Mushrooms do not make chlorophyll; mushrooms feed off dead and decomposing matter; we see only the fruit, not the body of the mushroom. 2. Mushrooms are used for cooking; mushrooms provide essential nutrients, such as copper, selenium and potassium; mushrooms provide B-complex vitamins. 3. Sample main ideas: Mushrooms are fungi not plants; Mushrooms taste good and are good for you.

Page 41: Picture Perfect

Possible answers:
1. The girl is sick with measles or chicken pox. Clues: thermometer, spots on face. 2. Haley is running in circles. Clue: Dog is chasing its tail. 3. Mary is waking up. Clue: Girl is yawning and stretching. 4. Clair and Rosa finished the race. Clue: Finish line ribbon.

Page 42: Guessing Games

1. John dropped some dishes. 2. It is afternoon; school is over. 3. Christina did not have enough money for three candy bars. 4. Mr. Juarez disturbed the bees' hive. 5. The birds ate the bread crumbs. 6. Luke rode his bike to the store.

Page 43: Take a Guess

1. The woman is a mail carrier. 2. She is delivering the mail. 3. Betty and Brenda are twins. 4. We know that Fiona is the oldest because the twins are her little sisters. 5. It is summer. 6. The McDonalds are going to the beach. 7. Sam's brother and father went fishing. 8. Sam says, "Not again" when he thinks they are having fish, so we can infer that they eat a lot of fish, probably because his father and brother like to go fishing a lot.

Page 44: Ugly Duckling or Swan?

1. The two stories told in the paragraph are "The Ugly Duckling" and a story about the author, Hans Christian Andersen. 2. Although we don't know for sure, we can infer that Andersen got the idea for this story from his own life.

Page 45: Jump to Conclusions

1. You might infer that no one is home. 2. You might infer that there is something on or under the sofa that your cat is really curious about. 3. You might infer that your brother ate the last cookie. 4. She might infer that someone was eating cookies in the living room. 5. He might infer that your mom is angry because he ate the cookies and dropped crumbs in the living room.

Page 46: Using What We Know

Possible answers:
1. Goldilocks had been walking for a long time through the woods. I know that walking for a long time can make someone hungry and tired. 2. Goldilocks jumped out of bed and ran all the way home when she heard the sound of the Bears' voices. Based on the story and what I know about being in a bear's territory, I think that Goldilocks was scared. 3. I know that bears can't really talk, that they don't really live in cottages, that they don't sleep in beds or cook porridge. Based on what I know, this story is a fantasy or a make-believe story.

Page 47: The New Neighbors

1. Her mother's purse and keys are on the table. 2. Sally's shoes are muddy. 3. Sally smells cookies baking. 4. The children must be younger because of their toys. 5. They might need a babysitter. 6. She likes cookies; she was hoping for someone her own age to move in next door; she wants a babysitting job (she is old enough to babysit).

Page 48: Supposing Scientists

1. Scientists might conclude that the tooth came from a poisonous dinosaur. 2. They know how the grooved tooth works in other poisonous animals. 3. They would have to guess that the dinosaur might or might not have been poisonous.

Page 49: Dinosaur Conclusions

1. The Oviraptor was a predator and was found with the eggs of another dinosaur. The scientists inferred that the Oviraptor was stealing the eggs. 2. The Oviraptor was not stealing, but protecting its own eggs.

Page 50: Ad Smart

1. The boy gained friends and happiness by drinking "Cool Cola." 2. The Smart Stuff Software helped the boy get a perfect report card. 3. Happy families eat "Happy Times Popcorn." 4. The dog is healthy and happy because of Good Puppy dog food.

Page 51: What Happens Next?

Possible answers:
2. The paint is going to spill because the man is falling. 3. The boy is going to sllip on the banana, because he is not looking where he is going. 4. The food is going to burn, because the woman is not paying attention.

Page 52: Predicting Patterns

1. white 2. blue square 3. The neighbor will probably wash his car. 4. Dad will be watching football on television. 5. Answers will vary.

Page 53: Title Clues

1. Mary 2. Mary 3. John 4. Mary 5. Mary 6. John 7. John 8. Mary 9. John 10. Mary

Page 54: Tippy Canoe

1. The counselor must have told them to wear life jackets, because Lin tells them that's what he said. 2. They might stand up in the canoe and tip it over. 3. They weren't listening to anything the counselor said.

Page 55: Predicting the Future

1. The ice cream will melt. Prior knowledge: Ice cream will melt in the sun or anywhere outside of a freezer. 2. The kitten gets away from the girl and maybe scratches her. Prior knowledge: Dogs chase cats 3. The driver would slam on the brakes. Prior knowledg: Kids follow balls into the street.

Page 56: Happy Endings

1. b. a fairy tale, because of the words "Once upon a time" and the King and Queen as typical fairy tale characters 2. It is typical for witches in fairy tales to be evil or wicked. 3. Probably the King should not go to the witch; he may cause even more trouble for himself. 4. You might be surprised since your prior knowledge of witches in fairy tales led you to assume that she would cause trouble.

Page 57: Lemonade for Sale!

1. More people are out enjoying leisure activities on Saturday. 2. People get thirsty on a hot summer day, especially if they are out exercising. 3. They will probably sell more as more people will be likely to come out as the day goes on. 4. People will go home, and they won't sell as much. They also might have to close up and go home. 5. The other children might get more customers. Meg and Millie might have to lower their price.

Page 58: Monkey Business!

1. The youngest monkey will reach for the bananas. 2. The monkeys will jump into the water hole to cool off.

Page 59: Fire!

1. more serious fires 2. to be taken out of a dangerous place 3. The fire might be less dangerous and/or easier to control. 4. because of the drought and the bark beetles 5. The fire will burn faster and be harder to control.

Page 60: Flood!

1. They will open the flood gates to let water drain out of the lake. 2. evacuate the people 3. Ideas may include the following: physical danger; lost or ruined possessions; irreplaceable items lost, such as photographs; nowhere to stay.

Page 61: Why Does It Happen?

Possible answers:
1. study 2. have a snack 3. do your chores 4. run fast 5. take your medicine 6. it will melt 7. they will die 8. you will get cavities 9. you will slip and fall 10. you won't learn anything

Page 62: Tell Me Why

1. she was stuck in a traffic jam 2. she has too much homework. 3. Brian lost his glove 4. it is raining 5. it's been raining for a week 6. the water is too cold

Page 63: Red Letter Words

Underlined words: because, Consequently, If…then, because, As a result, Due to, Because of

Page 64: Proverbs

1. If you don't waste things, then you won't be in need. 2. If you have good habits, then you will be successful. 3. If you save pennies, then you will always have money. 4. If you are in too much of a hurry, then things will go wrong. 5. If you work hard at something, then you will succeed. 6. If you keep trying, then you will find a way. 7. If all you care about is money, then you will not be happy.

Page 65: Family Feuds

1. because Jared made too much noise 2. Jared had to play with the baby. 3. because the family leaves the lights on 4. They will have to pay a fine for leaving the lights on.

Page 66: Because, Because, Because

1. in order to get home to Kansas 2. to ask for a brain 3. for a heart 4. for courage

Page 67: A Cause-Effect Move
1. The family moved away from their old town. 2. The children miss their friends; they had to leave their dog behind; the children miss going to the park with their old friends; they are sad; they are uncomfortable being the new students; their grades are not as high as they used to be; their mother is sad and worried that this experience is too difficult for her children.

Page 68: How Hurricanes Happen
Causes: Storms gather strength from warm ocean waters; warm air condenses to form storm clouds; converging winds collide and feed the cycle of warm air being pushed upward; warm air rising causes low pressure that causes strengthening winds as more air is drawn in.

Page 69: Disaster Relief
Effects: Hurricanes can cause death, destruction, pain, and suffering. Huge amounts of rain can cause flooding, which can strand people and damage property. Floods can also contaminate the water supply. Huge winds can blow down trees and buildings. Huge waves can cause flooding, property damage, and beach erosion.

Page 70: Stephen's Island Wren
The following words should be underlined: Since, so, Because, Since, so, Because, As a result. Causes: because it couldn't fly and wasn't used to predators; because the lighthouse keeper had a cat; because cats are predators

Page 71: Fact or Opinion?
1. F, O 2. F, O 3. O, F 4. F, O 5. O, O 6. F, O

Page 72: Finish the Facts
Possible answers:
1. planet 2. fruit 3. spring 4. winter 5. two 6. cold 7. gills 8. ocean 9. hot, a star 10. wings 11. gasoline 12. ten 13. nests 14. fly

Page 73: Opinions, Please
Answers should be opinions, not facts. Answers will vary.

Page 74: State Your Own . . .
Possible answers:
1. The sun is a star; the sun is beautiful. 2. Trees need sunlight; trees are splendid. 3. Winter is snowy; winter is fun. 4. Pizza is made with sauce and cheese on a flat dough; pizza is delicious. 5. My school is made of brick; my school is the best school in the state. 6. Basketball is played with two teams; basketball is boring. 7. George Washington was our first president; George Washington was a good general. 8. Sharks have sharp teeth; sharks are scary. 9. Babies cry when they are hungry; babies are too noisy. 10. The American Revolution was fought against the British army; the American Revolution was fought for good reasons.

Page 75: Fact Check
1. F 2. F 3. O 4. O 5. O 6. O 7. O 8. F 9. F 10. O 11. F 12. F 13. F 14. F 15. O

Page 76: Let's Go to the Movies
1. Maureen thinks space movies are boring. 2. Mac thinks monster movies are stupid. 3. Maureen uses the fact that The Blob got four stars from the Daily Review. 4. in the newspaper 5. He doesn't trust their opinions. 6. the fact that Space Warriors starts sooner; they won't have to wait around.

Page 77: Research the Facts
1. O 2. F 3. F 4. F 5. F 6. F 7. O 8. F 9. F 10. F 11. O 12. O 13. Dogs are useful animals. 14. Supporting facts: Dogs are used for hunting and companionship; some dogs work hard; watchdogs can help protect your home. 15. The fact that dogs like to bury bones does not support the topic sentence.

Page 78: A Trip to the Art Museum
1. F 2. O 3. O 4. F 5. F 6. O 7. F 8. The last sentence is a fact because it is a fact that critics said what they did about the artist; however, what was said was an opinion. Sarah is quoting the critics' opinion.

Page 79: Newspaper Facts
1. The lake was named "most polluted," it is no longer possible to swim in it, it is unsafe to use, wildlife populations have diminished; other sentences should be underlined. 2. There are other lakes nearby; other sentences should be underlined. 3. The first paragraph is the most persuasive; it has the most facts.

Page 80: Stamps of Approval
1. The following sentences should be underlined: *Everybody should have a hobby!* 2. The following two opinions should be underlined: *the cancellation marks add to the stamp's beauty; mint stamps are a better investment.*

Page 81: Sum It Up!
1. Ricky gets distracted and has trouble finishing his homework because of the goldfish on his desk. 2. Cindy and Phil both play instruments and want to be in a band together when they grow up.

Page 82: Summarizing Lists
1. In the junkyard they found used car parts. 2. It's fun to see farm animals. 3. I can recognize types of clouds. 4. I saw different forms of transportation. 5. I heard different languages spoken at the festival. 6. Tonight we have different desserts. 7. This book is about ocean life. 8. I want to learn about U.S. presidents.

Page 83: Summarizing Tiffany

1. The following chores should be underlined: washes dishes; vacuums; washes the car. Tiffany does chores to earn money. 2. Tiffany does household chores so she can earn money and buy her mother a gift. 3. The following phrases should be underlined: at night before going to bed; in the morning before breakfast; in the afternoon when she gets home from school. Tiffany reads all the time.

Page 84: Mary and Her Lamb

1. Mary had a lamb that followed her everywhere. 2. The lamb came to school, which was against the rules. 3. The teacher put the lamb outside where he waited for Mary. 4. The teacher tells the children that the lamb loves Mary because she loves the lamb.

Page 85: The Maine Idea

1. rocky coast; quaint villages; islands; mountains; clean, quiet lakes 2. explore villages, boat to islands and on lakes, climb mountains, swim, meet people 3. The second sentence is the best; it tells what the paragraph is mostly about.

Page 86: Pandas

1. yes 2. no 3. Pandas are endangered because their habitat (where bamboo grows) is being taken over and cut down by people. 4. yes 5. Pandas are endangered because their habitat (where bamboo grows) is being taken over and cut down by people.

Page 87: You're Invited

1. no 2. Jane thinks her birthday should be special because it's her twelfth birthday. 3. Jane is planning an extra-special party for her twelfth birthday and is inviting all her friends.

Page 88: You Be the Judge!

1. Max thinks Vic is a bad friend because he reported him to the teacher. 2. Vic thinks he was just doing his job and that Max shouldn't have been disobeying the rules. 3. Convincing argument could be that Max was not being a good friend by disobeying when it was Vic's responsibility to monitor students' behaviors.

Page 89: Movie Talk

Possible answers:

Main Idea: Movies should not replace books. The following details should be underlined: directors cut scenes, change endings, children miss out on dialogue, characters, and settings that are not in the movie but are in the book.

Summary: Movies of classic children's works should not be used as substitutes for the books. Children miss out on a lot when they don't read the original works.

Page 90: Get Your Peanuts!

Possible summaries:

1. Peanuts are not nuts, but an unusual type of legume. 2. Peanuts originated 5,000 years ago in South America and have since journeyed all over the globe and finally to North America. 3. Peanut butter is a nutritious and inexpensive source of protein that has been popular for over 100 years.

Page 91: Name That Category

1. These things are red. 2. These are all holidays. 3. These are ice-cream flavors. 4. These are card games.

Page 92: Match Them Up!

1. b 2. d 3. e 4. f 5. a 6. c

Page 93: Classify Animals

Mammals: whale, man, polar bear, dog, fox Reptiles: alligator, turtle, snake Arthropods: spider, caterpillar, ant, lobster Amphibians: frog, toad Birds: ostrich, robin, chicken, blue jay

Page 94: That's Classified

1. Furniture 2. Sporting Goods 3. Sporting Goods 4. Musical Instruments 5. Furniture 6. Pets and Pet Supplies 7. Pets and Pet Supplies 8. Jobs (Help Wanted) 9. Homes (Real Estate) 10. Automobiles

Page 95: Laundry Day

1. whites and darks 2. cold water and warm water 3. He will have four categories. 4. five piles

Page 96: Food Fun

Check that foods are in the correct categories. Discuss their selections of food.

Page 97: Planting a Garden

Tall plants: delphinium and sunflower. Medium plants: bachelor's buttons, daisy, and iris. Short plants: begonia, candytuft, and marigold.

Page 98: We Belong

Categories are listed; additional words will vary.

1. ocean mammals 2. sports 3. adjectives 4. family members 5. continents 6. vowels (or letters) 7. forms of transportation 8. children's book writers 9. office equipment 10. fruit

Page 99: The Category Game

Sample Names: Sam, Tim, Alicia, Paco, Len, Edward
Sample Birds: sandpiper, tern, albatross, parrot, lark, egret
Sample Foods: sandwich, tacos, apple, peanuts, lettuce, eggs
Sample Transportation: sleigh, tractor, automobile, plane, locomotive, elevator

Page 100: Wild or Tame

1. fox, antelope, panda, beaver, giraffe, tiger, eagle, blue jay, zebra, squirrel 2. pig, dog, horse, cat, rooster, cow, hamster, guinea pig, chicken, sheep 3. dog, cat, hamster guinea pig 4. pig, horse, rooster, cow, chicken, sheep

Page 101: They're Different

1. Basketball is played inside with a large orange ball and five people on a team; baseball is played outside with a small white ball, bats, and gloves and nine people on a side. 2. Summer is warm, with more hours of daylight and things growing; winter is colder, with shorter days, and everything dead or hibernating. 3. Apples are red or green; oranges are orange. Apples grow in colder climates; oranges need tropical temperatures. Oranges are citrus fruits; apples are not. 4. Lakes are calmer; oceans have tides and waves. Lakes have freshwater; oceans have salt water. 5. Cars are smaller than buses; buses make a lot of stops to pick up and let people off. 6. Talking uses the mouth; listening uses the ears. Talking is when you give your viewpoint; listening is when you listen to the viewpoint of others.

Page 102: Two Sisters

1.–3. they are hard-working, they love candy, and they are both good at counting money. 4.–5. Amelia is shy; Ellen is outgoing. Amelia is good at making candy; Ellen is not as good.

Page 103: Space Neighbors

1. Both Mars and Venus are neighbors of Earth. 2. Venus has an atmosphere; Mars does not. Venus is closer to the Sun than Mars. Mars has moderate temperatures; Venus is the hottest planet in the solar system. Venus has no moons, Mars has two. 3. Earth and Mars both have moderate temperatures and have at least one moon. 4. Earth and Venus are about the same size and both have atmospheres. 5. Earth supports life!

Page 104: Two Cities by the Bay

Boston: capital of the state, on the Atlantic Ocean, historic sites. *San Francisco:* on the Pacific Ocean, not the capital, hilly with cable cars. *Both:* quaint, colorful with interesting streets and beautiful old buildings. Both are on water and are important port cities. Both have historic charm and many cultural venues.

Page 105: Tomato Time

1. They are more different. 2. They grow to the same height. 3. Easy Red 4. Shady Lady is yellow/orange; Easy Red is deep red.

Page 106: Raccoons and Pandas

1. Raccoons are bold and outgoing; pandas are shy.
2. Humans are encroaching upon their habitats.

3. Raccoons are omnivorous so they can eat whatever is available, while pandas only eat one thing; also, raccoons are adaptable in a way that pandas are not.

Page 107: Pet Plans

1. parrot 2. puppy 3. parrot and puppy 4. lizard 5. rabbit and guinea pig 6. rabbit

Page 108: Making Choices

Possible answers:
One is about fun, the other about studying and learning; one has swimming lessons, the other has swimming fun; one orders pizzas and has barbecues, the other trains the campers to cook.

Page 109: Two Stories

1. They both feature an industrious, hardworking character and one who wastes time and doesn't prepare for the future. 2. In the first story the ant does not help the grasshopper; in the second story, the prairie mouse helps her cousin.

Page 110: City Mouse, Country Mouse

The following dangers of country life should be underlined: the hawk, the fox, shortage of food, difficulty getting food. The following discomforts of country life should be underlined: diet of berries, cold, damp hole. The following dangers of city life should be underlined: the cat The following discomforts of city life should be underlined: the Grandfather clock, constant diet of cheese, no fresh air. The follwing comforts of city life should be underlined: warm and cozy place to sleep; lots of cheese. The following comforts of country life should be underlined: fresh air, juicy berries, snug, little hole

Page 111: Map Adventures

1. by walking 2. at the lighthouse, Clear Pond, or Salt Pond 3. Mars Beach or Clear Pond 4. take the Tower Cut-off to Lighthouse Loop to the beach

Page 112: New England Map

1. six 2. Maine 3. New Hampshire and Massachusetts 4. Rhode Island 5. New Hampshire and Massachusetts 6. Vermont

Page 113: Matt's Goals

1. Yes, Monday was a perfect day for Matt. 2. He fed the cat and read for $\frac{1}{2}$ hour every day. 3. getting up with his alarm 4. 30 5. 22

Page 114: Mansfield Trees

1. ten 2. 0 3. 85 4. 40 5. pine 6. the roadside

Page 115: Graphic Artists

1. Monet, Monet 2. 100 3. 3 4. Van Gogh has become more popular. 5. about 38 6. Van Gogh might become more popular than Monet.

Page 116: Pizza Pie
1. 50% 2. 40% 3. 10% 4. yes 5. Students should put the correct symbols on the graph.

Page 117: For the Birds
1. sunflower 2. one 3. cardinal, chickadee, finch, nuthatch, sparrow, woodpecker 4. woodpecker 5. sugar water 6. finch

Page 118: Touchdown!
1. six 2. eight 3. fourteen 4. Sunday 5. three

Page 119: Sail Away
1. bow 2. stern 3. jib and mainsail 4. portholes 5. boom 6. keel

Page 120: The Moving Earth
1. convergent; because of the way the arrows are pointing 2. divergent 3. convergent 4. divergent

LITERARY ELEMENTS

Page 121: What Characters!
Possible answers:
1. kind, nice, generous 2. brave 3. greedy 4. slow, lazy, irresponsible 5. happy 6. bossy 7. honest 8. good, kind, nice, friendly, thoughtful 9. funny 10. smart, studious

Page 122: Oh, Those Pigs!
1. ungrateful; Fiddler is ungrateful because he doesn't seem to appreciate what Practical did for him. 2. greedy and selfish; Fifer wants the whole brick house to himself. 3. Practical is sensible, hardworking, kind, uncomplaining, and thoughtful. Students can find evidence in the story for the characteristics of Practical; for example, he is helpful, kind, and thoughtful to help his mother paint her door, and he is uncomplaining, even though he has his two brothers living in his house.

Page 123: Amanda Bean
1. It seems like the author does not want you to like Amanda, because she is described as a troublemaker and seems to be trying to ruin Tammy's birthday. 2. Amanda could be called selfish, inconsiderate, mean, but she might also be unhappy and insecure. 3. Selfish because she is only thinking of her own comfort; inconsiderate or mean to ruin Tammy's party. Sometimes, unhappy or insecure people act mean or selfish or inconsiderate.

Page 124: Four Sisters
1. Beth, contentedly 2. Meg wishes for new clothes; she is looking at her old dress. 3. They are too poor to have presents for Christmas. 4. Despite poverty and problems, the girls seem happy together. 5. Look for clues from the paragraph to support the answer. (*I like Beth because she seems happy with what she has*, or *I like Jo because she says what she is feeling very directly and honestly*).

Page 125: Where Are We?
1. We are in the country/mountains. 2. We are in the city. 3. Country images: birds, water, trees, sky, pine needle scent. City images: horns blaring, hard pavement, traffic, exhaust fumes, foods and flowers sold on street corners, people. 4. Choice of setting should be explained by what appeals to them from the paragraph.

Page 126: Set the Scene!
1. Dark, frowned, frozen, stripped, frost, black and ominous, vast silence, desolation, lifeless, lone, cold, savage, frozen-hearted 2. The Wild is treated like a character (frowning, leaning, frozen-hearted) and the author wants to show what a powerful force it is. 3. Probably not, because the landscape is like a character in the story, so you would be changing more than just the setting.

Page 127: Perfect Setting?
1. Setting description should include adjectives and phrases from the book. 2. There should be good reasons for why the setting is or is not important to the story (usually it is important in some way). 3.–4. Some settings are more interchangeable than others. A fairy tale often takes place in a generic imaginary kingdom, but it is the characters' actions that are most important, so the setting could be moved or modernized.

Page 128: Kansas or Oz?
1. Most students will probably choose Oz, especially in comparison to Kansas, because of the gorgeous scenery and birds and sparkling water. 2. Dorothy preferred Kansas to Oz, because she felt she belonged in Kansas with her family. (The answer to this could be subject to how familiar students are with the whole story. If they do not know that Dorothy missed her family, they could guess why she preferred Kansas).

Page 129: Plot Mountain
(Ascending) a. Prince invites ladies to ball. b. Stepmother won't let Cinderella go to the ball. c. Fairy Godmother appears. d. Prince dances and falls in love with Cinderella. (Climax, top) e. Cinderella runs off, leaving glass slipper. (Descending) f. Prince finds Cinderella. g. They get married and live happily ever after.

Page 130: Problems, Problems
1. Larry has the bully's watch, and the bully thinks Larry stole it. 2. Larry kept the watch instead of bringing it to the school office or the police station. 3. Larry could go right up to the bully and say, "I found your watch on the sidewalk," or he could bring the watch to the office right away.

Page 131: What If?
Possible answers:
1. What if Jack and his mother were not poor? 2. What if Jack sold the cow and got a good price for it as his mother wished? 3. What if the beans didn't grow or there were no giant's castle in the clouds? 4. Without conflict there is no story.

Page 132: Motivation
Student responses will vary.

Page 133: Sleepyhead!
1. 1 2. 3 3. 3 4. 1 5. 3 6. 3 7. 1 8. 3 9. 1 10. 3 11. 3 12. 1 13. 3 14. 1 15. 1 16. 3

Page 134: Who Is Speaking?
Fill in the lines as follows: Fred, Fred, John, Ben, Ben, John, Ben. 1. the author or narrator 2. third person 3. three 4. John and Fred 5. the twins' older brother

Page 135: Beach Vacation
1. A narrator is telling the story. No, the narrator is not in the story. 2. We learn about Ben, Bart, and Bonnie's thoughts. 3. Bonnie 4. no

Page 136: John and the Elf
We get only John's thoughts and point of view. For the elf's story, students need to be sure the voice is consistently first person.

Page 137: Name that Theme
1. apples 2. space, astronomy 3. poetry

Page 138: Theme Match
1. b 2. a 3. d 4. f 5. c 6. e

Page 139: Slow but Steady
1. The theme is "slow but steady wins the race."
2. *Possible answers:* The Boy Who Cried Wolf (Don't give false alarms.), The Dog in the Manger (Don't hoard what you can't use.)

Page 140: Team Theme
The following phrases should be underlined: working together as a team; that's how you win games; that's how you enjoy the game; that's how you become better players. Possible response: The theme is the importance of teamwork or of putting the team ahead of your own personal goals.

Page 141: Showing Emotion
1. happy, joyful, peaceful 2. tired, complaining 3. complaining, angry, bitter, upset (possibly joking) 4. angry, serious, upset 5. wistful, sad 6. sarcastic (possibly joking) 7. serious, urgent, cold, sarcastic, angry 8. eager, joyful, excited, happy 9. urgent, frightened 10. worried, upset

Page 142: Tone of Voice
The following words should be underlined: impatient, anxious, angrily, sarcastically, eagerly, happily, annoyed, complained, soothingly. 1. We know Amy doesn't mean that the situation is literally "great," because of the modifier, "angrily" that tells us her tone of voice. 2. Tim is being sarcastic. 3. Kelly's tone is peaceful, soothing, and happy.

Page 143: Author's Tone
1. The author's tone is light and amused. 2. The author portrays the king in a very positive way. The author doesn't seem to dislike the queen, but seems to feel more positive toward the king. The author is sympathetic to the queen.

Page 144: Nonfiction Tone
1. A 2. B 3. B 4. A 5. B 6. A

Page 145: What Is a Genre?
1. mystery 2. autobiography 3. fairy tale 4. science fiction 5. biography 6. historical fiction 7. fantasy 8. horror

Page 146: Why Do We Read?
1. F or NF; might read for enjoyment, for the love of language, for fun 2. NF; might be read out of interest in a character or time period, to learn something, for enjoyment 3. F; read for entertainment, enjoyment, interest in a particular time period 4. NF; look up word definitions 5. F; might be read for enjoyment, fun of solving a puzzle 6. F; read for information about other cultures, for entertainment 7. F; read for entertainment, use of imagination 8. F; read for entertainment, for the fun of being scared 9. NF; read to get information, research topics, narrow down topics, homework help 10. F; read for entertainment 11. NF; read for recipes or menu ideas 12. F; read for entertainment, use of imagination 13. NF; read for news and information. Answers will vary regarding Y and N answers.

Page 147: Librarian for a Day
1. e 2. c 3. d 4. f 5. g 6. a 7. b, h 8. i

Page 148: Thinking about Genre
1. fairy tale 2. newspaper editorial 3. fable 4. autobiography 5. myth/legend 6. cookbook 7. mystery 8. encyclopedia article

Page 149: A Day at the Fair
The following words should be underlined: sizzling, spicy, popping, buttery, sticky, sugary-sweet, clinging, dancing, breaking, pops, sailing, screaming, sweeps, shouting, feel (hot sun), jostling, juggling, tumbling. 1. spicy, sugary-sweet. 2. sticky, clinging, sweeps, feel, jostling 3. sizzling,

popping, breaking, pops, screaming, shouting 4. dancing, sailing, juggling, tumbling 5. spicy, buttery

Page 150: Painting with Words

1. B 2. The author uses such sense words as terrified, sweaty palms, pounding heart, sway under her feet, no words came out; all of these words convey how nervous Karla was. 3. In the first paragraph, Karla seems nervous at first, but she emerges as a self-confident, resilient character. In the second paragraph, the author's description makes it appear that she is more shy and fearful. Both words mean that Karla was afraid, but there are different shades of meaning. *Nervous* says she was worried. *Terrified* is more extreme and seems to convey a more intense experience of stage fright.

Page 151: Choosing the Mood

1. The mood is oppressive, stifling. 2. A hot wind would imply action and movement. 3. The mood is tense, fearful, suspenseful 4. If Clara were stifling a giggle, the mood would be more excited and playful, as if she were involved in a game of hide-and-seek instead of running from danger. 5. The mood is peaceful and serene. 6. If the night were eerily calm, it would add suspense and tension.

Page 152: Decisions, Decisions

1. Students will find more difficult words in paragraph A. 2. A is written in the third person; B is in the first person plural. B uses direct address. 3. A is more formal—longer words, third person, conventional sentence structure

Page 153: As Fast As a . . .

1. ice 2. wind 3. silk 4. apples 5. monkey 6. diamonds 7. drum 8. lion 9. desert 10. coal 11. candy 12. hornet

Page 154: Check It Out

1. Metaphor 2. Simile 3. Simile 4. Metaphor 5. Metaphor 6. Metaphor 7. Simile 8. Metaphor 9. Simile 10. Simile 11. Simile 12. Metaphor

Page 155: Hairy, Scary

1. exaggeration 2. The children, Mr. T., and Mrs. Ortiz all use hyperbole when they describe the spider. The following words should be underlined: huge, enormous, scary, hairy, monster, magnificent, monumental, monstrous. 3. Exaggeration can help bring attention to what you are trying to say.

Page 156: Person, Place, or Thing?

1. The stream or brook and the woods; the brook laughs and the stream whispers; the wood frowns and commands. 2. The idea is justice; justice blindly rules and sheds a goodly light. 3. birds, crickets, lantern 4. animals, plants, inanimate objects, abstract ideas

Page 157: Idioms

1. (d) Taking unnecessary chances 2. (f) Took a nap 3. (h) Extremely smart and quick 4. (l) Out of place 5. (n) Joking 6. (g) A narrow escape 7. (m) Avoiding the subject 8. (k) Eager to listen 9. (b) Count on uncertain things 10. (j) Stop working 11. (c) Eventually 12. (a) Annoys me 13. (e) Exaggerate the problem 14. (i) Unbelievable

RESEARCH SKILLS

Page 158: Spice Cabinet

Spices should be alphabetized: Allspice, Basil, Cardamom, Cinnamon, Cumin, Mace, Marjoram, Nutmeg, Oregano, Paprika, Tarragon, Thyme

Page 159: ABC's of the South

Southern states and cities alphabetized: 1. Alabama: Birmingham, Mobile, Montgomery; 2. Georgia: Atlanta, Augusta, Savannah; 3. Mississippi: Biloxi, Greenville, Jackson; 4. North Carolina: Charlotte, Greensboro, Raleigh; 5. South Carolina: Charleston, Columbia, Spartanburg; 6. Tennessee: Knoxville, Memphis, Nashville

Page 160: Presidential ABC's

Bush G., Bush, G. W., Carter, Clinton, Coolidge, Eisenhower, Ford, Harding, Hoover, Johnson, Kennedy, McKinley, Nixon, Reagan, Roosevelt, F. D., Roosevelt, T., Taft, Truman, Wilson

Page 161: Winter and Summer

Winter: alpine skiing, bobsled racing, cross-country skiing, figure skating, ice hockey, luge, ski jumping, snowboarding, speed skating. *Summer:* archery, baseball, canoeing, cycling, gymnastics, high diving, horseback riding, rowing, sailing, swimming, tennis, track and field, volleyball.

Page 162: Using the Dictionary

1. conjunction, preposition, or adverb 2. buttery 3. burn 4. two

Page 163: Dictionary Practice

1. They are different because one is for grazing, the other a seed-bearing crop. They are alike because they are both plants. 2. They are more alike than different, because the first two have to do with a rubbing motion and the third definition is an abstraction of that, as in someone rubbing you the wrong way. 3. *Grate* is listed twice because there are two definitions that are not related. The two definitions of *grass* describe variations of the plants. Possible sentences: 4. I will grate some cheese. 5. He looked through the iron grate into the secret garden.

Page 164: Pronounce It

1. *Above, glove,* and *love* rhyme; *cove, grove,* and *rove* also rhyme. 2. *Move* does not rhyme with any of the other words.

Page 165: Look It Up!

The following words should be circled: bowling, famous, foreign, capital, district, lily, extra, bingo, library, palace, navy, punctual, elevator, carp. 1. blare, bleed, blemish; 2. carriage, carrot; 3. delirious, delta, delude; 4. engage, engine, entity; 5. formal, formidable; 6. larkspur, latent; 7. nettle, nickel, nightingale; 8. protein, prove, pun

Page 166: A Little Quiz

1. d 2. c 3. d 4. d 5. d 6. c

Page 167: Preview and Predict

1. fiction 2. seventeen 3. about 300 4. First person; because of the use of "I" and "My" in the chapter titles. 5. pirates and treasure hunts 6. Look for reasons based on information gained from the table of contents. (*I would like to read this book because I like adventure stories.*)

Page 168: Lost Contents

1. math textbook 2. newspaper 3. social studies textbook 4. mystery book 5. cookbook

Page 169: Using a Table of Contents

1. science textbook 2. Unit three is the longest, because it has the greatest number of pages. 3. more than 433 4. page 26 5. page 374 (the Glossary)

Page 170: Using an Index

1. a math textbook 2. alphabetical order 3. Money 4. a. page 130 b. page 41 c. pages 15, 101 d. pages 8–9 and 121–122 e. pages 219–221 f. pages 111–112

Page 171: Busy, Busy Librarian

1. Four types of indexes are mentioned. 2. Yes, so different types of information can be easily accessed. For instance, a social studies text might have an index of topics, an index of important dates, and an index of maps. 3. Mrs. Klingman can teach people how to use indexes so they can help themselves. 4. a. Topics b. Author Index c. Maps d. Topics

Page 172: Knowledge Collections

1. I 2. IV 3. I 4. I 5. III 6. V 7. II 8. VIII

Page 173: CD-ROM Power!

1. LIN 2. LEW 3. LAT 4. LEW 5. LEM 6. LON 7. LIN 8. LYD

Page 174: Good Work, Joe!

1. She was pleased with Joe's topic because it had something to do with the Civil War, and it focused on one aspect of the war. 2. The topic was too narrow. 3. The topic was too broad. 4. The encyclopedia helped Joe focus on one aspect of the Civil War. It helped him see if there was too much or not enough information to write a paper.

Page 175: Types of Encyclopedias

1. c 2. h 3. k 4. e 5. g 6. l 7. i 8. d 9. f 10. b 11. j 12. a

Page 176: What Are Almanacs?

1. SA 2. W 3. PA 4. WA 5. W 6. WA 7. PA 8. SA

Page 177: Mystery Tides

1. two high and two low 2. Friday, Saturday, Sunday, or Monday 3. The clue can only be found on Monday, when low tide coincides with sunrise.

Page 178: Thesaurus Time

Possible answers:

1. The teacher said the book was *excellent*. 2. He is a *well-behaved* boy. 3. She is so *agreeable*. 4. It is a *lovely* day. 5. That movie was *entertaining*. 6. Oh, school is so *unexciting*.

Page 179: Atlases for All

1. astronomy or stargazing 2. world atlas 3. physical map 4. street atlas 5. The political map would be more likely to change. 6. sky atlas

Page 180: Which One to Use?

1. b 2. e 3. a 4. i 5. g 6. h 7. d 8. e 9. f or e 10. d 11. d 12. c or e

Share Your Bright Ideas

We want to hear from you!

Your name_____Date_____

School name_____

School address_____

City _____State _____Zip_____Phone number (_____)_____

Grade level(s) taught_____Subject area(s) taught_____

Where did you purchase this publication?_____

In what month do you purchase a majority of your supplements?_____

What moneys were used to purchase this product?

_____School supplemental budget _____Federal/state funding _____Personal

Please "grade" this Walch publication in the following areas:

Quality of service you received when purchasing .... A B C D

Ease of use.. A B C D

Quality of content.. A B C D

Page layout .... A B C D

Organization of material .... A B C D

Suitability for grade level .... A B C D

Instructional value... A B C D

COMMENTS:_____

_____

What specific supplemental materials would help you meet your current—or future—instructional needs?

_____

Have you used other Walch publications? If so, which ones?_____

May we use your comments in upcoming communications? _____Yes _____No

Please **FAX** this completed form to **888-991-5755**, or mail it to

Customer Service, Walch Publishing, P. O. Box 658, Portland, ME 04104-0658

We will send you a **FREE GIFT** in appreciation of your feedback. **THANK YOU!**